Herbrand Arthur Russell Bedford

A great Agricultural Estate

Being the Story of the Origin and Administration of Woburn and Thorney

Herbrand Arthur Russell Bedford

A great Agricultural Estate
Being the Story of the Origin and Administration of Woburn and Thorney

ISBN/EAN: 9783337280871

Printed in Europe, USA, Canada, Australia, Japan

Cover: Foto ©Suzi / pixelio.de

More available books at **www.hansebooks.com**

A GREAT

AGRICULTURAL ESTATE

BEING THE STORY OF
THE ORIGIN AND ADMINISTRATION OF
WOBURN AND THORNEY

BY THE DUKE OF BEDFORD

'The improvement of the ground is the most natural obtaining
of riches, for it is our great mother's blessing, the earth; but it is
slow: and yet, where men of great wealth do stoop to husbandry,
it multiplieth riches exceedingly'—BACON

SECOND EDITION

LONDON
JOHN MURRAY, ALBEMARLE STREET
1897

PREFACE

THE speech made by me at Thorney on May 13, 1896, attracted such widespread attention that I have been urged to give some further details on the subject with which it dealt. The material which I have collected is very voluminous, and the subject on which I am writing may be regarded as almost inexhaustible, if it is to be investigated in all its details and ramifications. The leisure on which I had counted was lost by an accident, and I have been forced to crowd into two months, work to which full justice could only be done in a much longer time. But the facts and figures contained in the following pages will, I believe, be intelligible to all who are interested in the question of estate management, whether directly or indirectly.

B.

May 1, 1897.

CONTENTS

THE STORY

OF A

GREAT AGRICULTURAL ESTATE

———◦◦◦———

INTRODUCTORY

A word of explanation may be required as to
the reasons for publishing the facts and figures
contained in this little book.

On May 13, 1896, when presiding at a
meeting of the Thorney Unionist Association,
I delivered a speech on questions affecting the
welfare of the three classes interested in the
Thorney Estate. Landlord, tenant farmers and
labourers being present on that occasion, the
opportunity was taken to review the history of
the estate for eighty years, and to show—as
far as the limits of a speech would allow—that,
while the circumstances of the labourers had
improved, taxation both local and imperial had

B

increased ; that rent [1] had disappeared, not only from Thorney, but also from the Bedfordshire and Buckinghamshire estates ; and that the possession of these properties, even after excluding all expenditure on the Abbey, park, and farm, at Woburn, now involved upon their owner a heavy annual loss. I further attempted to show how none of the responsibility generally regarded as inseparable from the position of a great land-owner had been evaded, even though the burden borne by the one individual person connected with Thorney who obtained nothing from it, was only recompensed by the feeling that he was instrumental in maintaining a system which in the past has added, and in the present is still adding, to the welfare of thousands.

This speech attracted more public attention than I expected, and was commented on by the press of all shades of political opinion. In these circumstances I was advised, by friends on whose judgment I rely, to state my case

[1] Cf. Mill's *Political Economy*, book ii. cap. xvi. par. 3, p. 257, ed. 1868.

in some less ephemeral form than that of a village speech. Acting upon this suggestion, I began to collect material for an article in one of the Reviews. But I soon discovered that, even if the case were presented with the utmost conciseness, it could not be compressed within the limits of a contribution to a monthly or quarterly magazine. So much for the origin of this book.

The 'Story of a Great Estate' not only contains facts which may tend to weaken the force of arguments commonly advanced by some ardent land reformers. It also, I hope, proves that the system of land tenure which allows a great estate to descend unimpaired from one generation to another, secures to those dwelling on the soil material and moral advantages greater than any that are promised under any alternative system, tried or untried. I have the less hesitation in speaking of the principle of dealing with tenants and cottagers on the Bedford Estate, because that principle has been adopted for generations. The system, be it good or bad, existed long before I succeeded to the property. Whatever its value or defects, it was not created by me; and, therefore, any favourable conclusions, which may be drawn from the facts and figures given in this book, reflect on me no credit.

The system adopted on the Bedford Estate is not a recent creation. On the contrary, it is a social structure tested by stress of change, and ratified by the experience of many lives. Against it may be opposed theoretical remedies, which are advocated by their supporters as infallible; but, in this country at least, they have never been practically tested for an hour, and on their efficacy no adequate opinion can be formed until they have been in operation for at least a century. So long as the English race retains its characteristic and cautious deliberation in the acceptance of radical change, it will scarcely reject the results of tested experience for the most attractive theories which have never proved their promises by their fruits.

Every one admits that public interests override the interests of individuals. Judged by this test, the 'Story of a Great Estate' will possibly be found to demonstrate the service done to the country by the working of the existing system. If the accumulation of large areas of land in few hands is an evil, it is incumbent upon those who seek to prevent it by legislation to show that their proposals will result in the establishment of a system more advantageous to the general community than that which now exists. It is not fair to draw distinctions on the score of ownership between real and personal property. As a subsequent chapter will show, the money invested in the reclamation of Thorney from the fens and money invested in the funds are equally the fruit of industry; both investments are therefore equally entitled to protection by the State. Rights legally acquired under existing land laws cannot be disturbed without detriment to that indefinable sentiment of security which may easily be destroyed, but can neither be restored nor created by legislation. Confidence is the vital breath of nations, and to no class in a nation is it more vital than to that which depends for livelihood upon its labour.

The survey of the history of a great estate, which for centuries has been held continuously by the same family, no less than the study of the history of the laws affecting the land, indicate that general changes cannot be immediately effected in the occupation, nor even in the cultivation, of the soil. Relief from agricultural depression accordingly must be sought, not in the extermination of the great landlord; nor in the artificial manufacture of a peasant proprietary without either capital, or hereditary aptitude in the management of land; nor in protection; nor in the production of cabbages, jam, eggs, ducks or fruit. A principal source of relief to agricultural depression is to be found in the restoration of confidence and the consequent attraction of more capital into land; in the encouragement of good farming; and in the obliteration of such barriers to the wider distribution of landed interests as are raised by the existing artificial and costly system of land transfer. If confidence in the sanctity of private property in land were absolutely restored, energies that are now paralysed would be attracted to the soil, and the way would at least be prepared for the partial rehabilitation of British agriculture.

Now that commerce has ceased to expand with sufficient rapidity to employ a growing population, the exclusive privileges of the few large landowners are discussed with deepening eagerness. The assailants of property may be noisy out of all proportion to their numbers ; their confidence may rest on ignorance rather than on reason or experience, and they may forget that the first victims of economic blunders are the poor; but it is now too late to ignore the dangers of an agitation which has been encouraged by recent Finance Legislation. A cry has been raised which has already scared away capital from the land. It has done even more than this. It has raised misgivings in the minds of those who, in point of income, would positively gain by casting off the burden of heavily taxed agricultural property, and by giving up a possession which not only involves the owner, who does his duty, in a considerable annual loss, but exposes him to the odium and anxieties attaching to ownership of land. An agitation has been set on foot, and assiduously encouraged by political leaders, that landlords are a parasitical class, feasting on others' labour, reaping where others sow ; and that it is the national duty of the State not to defend their rights like those of other citizens, but to eradicate them as vermin whose existence is incompatible with public welfare. Political leaders have industriously fostered the misconceptions, that English land tenure is a solitary exception to the rule of European land-holding, and that, so long as the present system is allowed to remain, the people are excluded from advantages which would be theirs if once the system were abolished by a reforming Parliament. Readers of the following pages will be enabled to judge how far these views are borne out by the Story of the Bedford Estate.

The management of an estate may be tested from the point of view of the landlord, the tenant, or the labourer. But if we ask what form of land tenure is the best, the answer can only be given by ascertaining which of them practically contributes most to the sum of national prosperity. No one wishes to deny that the spontaneous increase of small owners is socially and politically valuable, or that the wholesale absorption of the properties of yeomen into the great estates may be a source of social and political danger. But the process by which large landed properties grew has almost universally ceased to work. The 'Story of a Great Estate,' at least, will show that, for the greater part of a century, there has been little or no augmentation of its acreage. Thorney and Woburn are substantially of the same area to-day as they were two hundred and fifty years ago.

If the effect on the general prosperity be the test of rival systems, it will be admitted that the owner of a great estate is in a better position to contribute to the welfare of the people on that estate than are the smaller proprietors. He is better able to withstand a fall in prices or an adverse season; he can help deserving tenants at a pinch, and assist them to tide over bad times. He has, as a rule, more capital; it is expended more systematically; there is more economy of labour and material; improvements are carried on in a better directed and more far-reaching way; the sources of profit, for all but the owner, are usually more diversified in kind as well as in

number ; and above all, there is continuity of
management.

The Land question, then, stripped of its
local and particularist meanings, I understand
to include the respective interests of owners,
occupiers, and cultivators, and the bearing of
those interests on the public welfare.   Farmers
and landlords may differ on some questions ;
but they agree that the seasons have been
adverse and prices deplorable; that land is
exorbitantly taxed;   that railway rates are
an English bounty on foreign produce ; and
that hired labour is scarce, and perhaps not
of the same quality as formerly.   The agricultural labourer has, in most places, his own
special grievance.   He complains, and perhaps
justly, that for him there is no rung on the
social ladder on which he can place his foot.
Add to all this the sense of insecurity produced
by class legislation which scares capital from
the land, and we have a chain of circumstances
which clanks aloud at Bacon's grim jest—
'Where men of great wealth do stoop to husbandry, it multiplieth riches exceedingly.'

If much of the land be unsaleable and half

farmed, some part of the responsibility lies at the door of politicians who advocate legislative changes behind which looms the ominous prospect of confiscation.   No business man will embark capital in the purchase or improvement of land if the money invested in either is to fall into other hands when the wild proposals for the compulsory distribution of property are realised.

CHAPTER I

HISTORICAL

1486–1895

It may be interesting to trace the growth of the Bedford system of estate management, to which constant allusion is made in these pages, and to find the heads of the Russell family, from generation to generation, devoting their energies to the development of their landed estates, and to agriculture and gardening.

A brief retrospect of the family history will show that from the time of the third Earl the Russells have identified themselves with the improvement of the soil. Landscape gardening, reclamation of fen land, arboriculture, high farming and stock breeding, housing of agricultural labourers, education of the rural population, and experimental farms form the history of the race in connection with the lands they owned.

John Russell, the first Earl of Bedford, was sprung from an old Norman family, well established in the West Country at the commencement of the thirteenth century. His father and grandfather are buried in Swyre Church, Dorset. John Russell had travelled, was a linguist and a man of varied accomplishments.

In 1506, when the Archduke Philip was cast by a storm upon the English coast in the neighbourhood of Weymouth, John Russell, who was then residing in Dorsetshire, was sent for by his uncle, Sir Thomas Trenchard, then Governor of the Coast, to assist in the entertainment of the illustrious visitor. No time was lost in informing the King (Henry VII.) of the arrival of so important a foreign prince in England. King Henry invited Philip to Windsor, and the Archduke took Russell with him and spoke warmly to the King of his talents and character. Thereafter his rise was rapid and steady, Henry VII. making him a Gentleman of the Privy Chamber.

Henry VIII. held Russell in high esteem, and employed him on all his most important diplomatic negotiations. He was continually abroad, accompanying King Henry on all his French wars, and was sent by him to Geneva, Rome, Naples, Milan, and Venice. He lost an eye by an arrow at the siege of Morlaix, took part in the battle of Pavia, and was present at the Field of the Cloth of Gold.

In 1547 some eight years before his death, Edward VI. granted him, in addition to lands previously conferred by Henry VIII. in France, the Cistercian Abbey of Woburn,[1] and in 1549 the Abbey of Thorney; but there is no record of his ever having lived at Woburn or having visited Thorney.

The only personal part which the first Earl of Bedford appears to have taken in the dissolution of the monasteries was an interposition with Cromwell in behalf of Peterborough Abbey, which led to the revenues of

---

[1] It is interesting to note that the value of the grant of Woburn Abbey made at the visitation in 1525, was estimated at 391l. 18s. 2d. per annum.

that Abbey alone being settled on the bishopric
of the same name.[2]

Francis, the second Earl, although Sheriff
of Bedfordshire at the age of nineteen, and
M.P. for Buckinghamshire,[3] spent a great part
of his early life in France with his father.
During the reign of Mary he found it prudent
to retire to Geneva, but on the accession of
Elizabeth he returned to England and was
appointed Governor of Berwick.

It was to him that Ruthven fled after the
murder of Rizzio, and it was from the account
of this eye-witness that Bedford wrote the
despatch to the Lords of the Council describing the scene at Holyrood.

In 1572 the second Earl of Bedford, then in
London, writes in dismay to Lord Burleigh at
the prospect of a visit to Woburn from Queen
Elizabeth. It should be remembered that in
those days Woburn Abbey was ill-fitted for
the reception of Royalty. The original letter
is as follows :

[2] Cf. *Great Governing Families of England*, vol. ii. p. 29.

[3] The first instance of an eldest son of a peer being elected to sit in the House of Commons.

'I am now going to prepare for her Ma^tie^s
coming to Woborne, which shall be done in
the best and most hastiest manner that I can.
I trust y^r L^p will have in remembrance to provide helpe that her Mat^s tarrieng be not above
two nights and a daye, for, for so long tyme do
I prepare. I pray God, the Rowmes and Lodg-
ings there may be to her Mat^s contentacion
for the tyme. If I could make them better
upon such a sodeyn, then would I, be assured,
they should be better than they be. So w^t my
hartie thanks to your good L. remayning
always, as I have just cause, yo^rs, and so
commit you to God's keeping. From Russell
House this xvi^th of July, 1572.

> 'Y^r L. right assured,

> > 'F. BEDFORD.'

He was godfather to Sir Francis Drake, and
founded the Free School at Woburn.

Edward, the third Earl of Bedford, was
neither statesman, soldier, nor diplomatist.
He succeeded at the age of eleven, and died
young. In earlier life he is mentioned as
shining in tilts and tourneys, but in his later

years he was crippled by a fall, out hunting. He was so bruised against a tree that he was thought to be dead.[4]

It would appear that an attempt was made to draw him into the Earl of Essex's insurrection in 1603, as will be seen from the following extract from his statement to the Lords of the Council:

'From Alderman Holyday's house,
'Feb. 14.

'It was after ten o'clock, prayers and sermon begun, that the Lady Rich came to my house and told me that the Earl of Essex desired to speak with me: upon which I went with her in her coach, none of the family following me out of the sermon-room, and I going unknown to my family. About eleven o'clock I came to Essex House, where, shortly after, the Earl of Essex with others of his company drew themselves into secret conference, whereto I was not called, nor made acquainted with any thing, but only of some danger which the Earl of Essex said he was in, by the practice of some private enemies.

[4] Cf. *Court and Times of James I.* vol. i.

C

Howbeit I, doubting that that course tended to some ill, and the rather suspecting it for that I saw not my uncle Sir William Russell there, presently desired to convey myself away; and for that purpose withdrew myself so far, that I neither heard anything of the Earl of Essex's consultation nor yet of the speeches with the Lords of the Council. From that time I endeavoured to come from the Earl of Essex so far as I might with safety, and to that end severed myself from him at a cross-street end : and, taking water, before I heard any proclamation, came back to my house about one o'clock; where I made no delay, but with all convenient speed put myself and followers in readiness : and with the best strength I could then presently make, being about the number of twenty horse, I went toward the Court for her Majesty's service.'

He and the Countess of Bedford appear to have been somewhat in advance of their time in horticulture. The following extract from Sir William Temple [5] describes their garden at Moor Park in Hertfordshire :

> *Works of Sir William Temple.* Fol. 1720, vol. i. p. 170.

'The perfectest figure of a garden I ever saw, either at home or abroad, was that of Moor Park in Hertfordshire, which I knew thirty years ago. It was made by the Countess of Bedford, esteemed among the greatest wits of her time, and celebrated by Doctor Donne : and with very great care, excellent contrivance, and much cost ; but greater sums may be thrown away without effect or honour if there want sense in proportion to money, or if nature be not followed : which I take to be the great rule in this, and perhaps in every thing else, as far as the conduct not only of our lives, but our Governments. And whether the greatest of mortal men should attempt the forcing of nature may best be judged by observing how seldom God Almighty does it Himself, by so few and undisputed miracles as we see or hear of in the world. For my own part I know not three wiser precepts for the conduct either of princes or private men, than *Servare modum, finemque tueri, naturamque sequi.*

'Because I take the garden I have named to have been in all kinds the most beautiful and perfect, at least in the figure and disposition, that I have ever seen, I will describe it for a model to those that meet with such a situation, and are above the regards of common. expence. It lies on the side of a hill (on which the house stands), but not very steep. The length of the house, where the best rooms and of most use or pleasure are, lies upon the breadth of the garden ; the great parlour opens into the middle of a terras gravel-walk that lies even with it, and which may be, as I remember, about three hundred paces long, and broad in proportion : the border set with standard laurels, and at large distances, which have the beauty of orange-trees, out of flower and fruit : from this walk are three descents by stone steps, in the middle and at each end, into a very large parterre : this is divided into quarters by gravel walks and adorned with two fountains and eight statues in the several quarters : at the end of the terras-walk are two summer-houses, and the sides of the parterre are ranged with two large cloisters open to the garden, upon arches of stone, and ending with two other summer-houses even

with the cloisters, which are paved with stone
and designed for walks of shade, there being
none other in the whole parterre. Over these
two cloisters are two terrasses covered with
lead, and fenced with balusters : and the
passage into these airy walks is out of the
two summer-houses at the end of the first
terras-walk. The cloister facing the south is
covered with vines and would have been
proper for an orange-house, and the other for
myrtles, or other more common greens : and
had I doubt not been cast for that purpose, if
this piece of gardening had been then in as
much vogue as it is now.

'From the middle of the parterre is a
descent by many steps flying on each side of a
grotto that lies between them (covered with
lead and flat) into the lower garden, which is
all fruit trees ranged about the several quarters
of a wilderness which is very shady : the walks
here are all green, the grotto embellished with
figures of shell rockwork, fountains, and water-
works. If the hill had not ended with the
lower garden, and the wall were not bounded
by a common way that goes through the park,

they might have added a third quarter of all greens ; but this want is supplied by a garden on the other side of the house, which is all of that sort, very wild, shady, and adorned with rough rockwork and fountains.

'This was Moor Park when I was acquainted with it, and the sweetest place, I think, that I have seen in my life, either before or since, at home or abroad : what it is now I can give little account, having passed through several hands that have made great changes in gardens as well as houses ; but the remembrance of what it was is too pleasant ever to forget, and there-fore I do not believe to have mistaken the figure of it, which may serve for a pattern to the best gardens of our manner, and that are most proper for our country and climate.'

Francis, the fourth Earl,[6] and his successor earnestly and continuously applied themselves to the task of developing their landed estates, as will be seen from the following chapter.

---

[6] Grandson of Francis, second Earl and son of Sir William Russell, who was Governor of Flushing and Lord Deputy of Ireland, and to whom Sir Philip Sydney be-queathed his gilt armour on the battlefield of Zütphen.

Earl Francis was succeeded in 1641 by his son William, fifth Earl and afterwards first Duke of Bedford, who served on the side of the Parliament, commanding their cavalry at the battle of Edgehill. But in 1643, weary of the war, he abandoned the Parliamentary cause and went to the King at Oxford.

For this desertion the Parliament sequestrated his estates; but at the end of 1643, in a letter to the Speaker of the House of Lords, he explained his conduct as dictated by a desire to induce his Majesty to comply with the demands of his Parliament, 'for which purpose I went to Oxford, but, perceiving the fruitlessness of the attempt, I resolved thenceforth whatsoever prejudice might befall me thereby to cast myself wholly on the mercy of the Parliament.'

Bedford was in custody for a few days, but in July 1644 the sequestration was taken off the estates.

According to Macaulay, the fifth Earl of Bedford accepted the dukedom with some reluctance, alleging, as a reason for preferring his earldom to a dukedom, that an earl who had a numerous family might send one son to the Temple, and another to a counting house in the City, but the sons of a duke were all lords, and a lord could not make his bread either at the Bar or on 'Change.

Wriothesley, second Duke, was Lord Lieutenant of Bedfordshire and Cambridgeshire, and is mentioned by Lord Orford, in an account given by him of a visit to Woburn, as having improved his park and grounds and having earned the reputation of a great husbandman. He appears to have been devoted both to floriculture and agriculture.

In a letter to Sir Hans Sloane [7] he seeks to tempt him to come to Woburn by stating that he was about to receive a great number of rarities, and particularly a large collection of ranunculi from Candia, such a one as he believes was never before seen in England.

Wriothesley, second Duke, died young. His son Wriothesley, third Duke, succeeded

---

[7] The Physic Garden conveyed by Sir Hans Sloane to the Apothecaries' Company still exists in Chelsea. It was 'for the manifestation of the power and wisdom and goodness of God in creation, and that the apprentices might learn to distinguish good and useful plants from hurtful ones.'

him when only three years of age, but dying
at the age of twenty-four, he was in turn
succeeded by his brother John, fourth Duke.
John, though an active politician, at the
same time delighted in a country life, and
his handiwork is everywhere apparent at
Woburn Abbey, which was almost entirely re-
built by him on a plan of great extent. He
took an especial interest in planting. The
wood now known at Woburn as the Ever-
greens was planted by him in 1743 with
various kinds of pines and firs, selected with
the assistance of Philip Miller [8] and thinned by
his own care. On this last point an anecdote
is related characteristic of his disposition.
The Duke perceiving that the plantation required thinning in order to admit a free circu-
lation of air and give health and vigour to the
young trees, gave instructions to his gardener,
and directed him as to the mode and extent of
the thinning required. The gardener paused
and hesitated, and at length said: ' Your

[8] Gardener and botanist,
born in 1691. He succeeded
his father as gardener to the
Company of Apothecaries at
Chelsea, and soon distin-
guished himself by his knowledge of plants.

Grace must pardon me if I humbly remon-
strate against your orders, but I cannot
possibly do what you desire ; it would at once
destroy the young plantation, and moreover it
would be seriously injurious to my reputation
as a planter.' The Duke replied, 'Do as I
desire you, and I will take care of your reputation.' The plantation was consequently
thinned according to his instructions, and the
Duke caused a board to be fixed in the plantation, facing the road, on which was inscribed,
' This plantation has been thinned by John,
Duke of Bedford, contrary to the advice and
opinion of his gardener.'

We are so accustomed to Agricultural
shows and Agricultural societies ; so used to
the pleasurable contemplation of our fine
breeds of cattle and sheep and our well-tilled
fields, that we can hardly realise the fact that
England as an agricultural country left much
to be desired at the end of last century.
Francis, fifth Duke of Bedford, did realise this
fact, and was among the first to initiate an
agricultural system which was destined, some
years later, to make the agricultural industry

of Great Britain a model for the whole civilised world. He founded a local agricultural society, started a model farm of three hundred acres, and inaugurated the once well-known Woburn sheep shearings.[9] These meetings, at which hundreds of the men who were most distinguished in agriculture assembled, covered much of the ground now occupied by the Royal Agricultural Society. We find the same programme. Though sheep breeding was of especial interest, Duke Francis gave prizes for cattle, sheep, and ploughing competitions. We read of Mr. Pickford's pig which weighed about 100 stone ; of a fat three-year-old wether of the New Leicester breed, 296 lbs. live weight; and of another three-year wether, on the loin of which ' the fat measured seven inches.'

Implements were exhibited and tried, and there was a special reason why Woburn should be the seat of such experiments, since the surveyor to the Dukes of Bedford from 1790 to

[9] A charming account of these meetings is given in Mr. Ernest Clarke's paper, ' Agriculture and the House of Russell,' vol. ii. (3rd series) of the *Journal of the Royal Agricultural Society* (1891).

1821 was Robert Salmon, a man of remarkable inventive genius, who gave to the world improvement after improvement.

It is curious to find Duke Francis in 1797 conducting experiments in the feeding of cattle and the growing of grasses—experiments which the Royal Agricultural Society is still conducting on the Woburn Estate in 1897.

As Duke Francis died young, in 1802, he never had the intense satisfaction of seeing the results of his exertions. Mr. Bennett, in an essay on the Farming of Bedfordshire, speaks of these 'efforts to arouse the torpor-stricken agriculturists of his day.' I notice that there were in 1857 'scores of farms producing 50 per cent. more corn than in 1794, and supplying the metropolitan markets with a stone of meat for every pound supplied at the former period.'

Though young, Duke Francis was appreciated by his compeers. The Board of Agriculture, 'in common with every friend to the improvement of the country, lamented the death of the most judicious and munificent promoter of the national agriculture in all its branches.' The well-known and observant Arthur Young was equally eulogistic :

'The agricultural world never perhaps sustained a greater individual loss than the husbandry of this Empire has suffered by the death of the Duke of Bedford.'

.   .   .   .   .

'In July 1795 I passed four days at Woburn and there found many signs of a decided attention to agricultural pursuits. The first [1] sheep-shearing celebrated by a numerous company was in June 1797, and continued to be held in the same month every succeeding year, but with increasing numbers and *éclat*, till it became at last by far the most respectable agricultural meeting ever seen in England, that is, in the whole world—attended by nobility, gentry, farmers and graziers from various parts of the three Kingdoms, from many countries in Europe, and also from America. Through all this period the Duke

[1] It is due to Sir John Sinclair, founder and first President of the Board of Agriculture, to note that the first sheep-shearing festival was held at Queensferry, near Edinburgh, in 1791.

was advancing rapidly the improvements of his great farm ; increasing and wonderfully ameliorating the breeds of live stock, in which he was singularly skilled and highly successful in all his exertions.'

From its foundation up to the date of his death Duke Francis officiated as President of the Smithfield Club.

In this office he was succeeded by his brother John, sixth Duke, who loyally maintained the agricultural traditions of Woburn. The sheep-shearing meetings increased in popularity and importance ; but in 1821 the Duke having come to the conclusion that the objects of the Smithfield Club had been accomplished withdrew from it, and ultimately discontinued the Woburn sheep-shearings, which had also served their purpose by bringing into existence numerous agricultural societies.

In 1838 the Duke became Governor of the English Agricultural Society, and held office as Vice-President until his death in 1839.

Francis, seventh Duke, more than maintained the family traditions, and his name is still fresh in the counties with which he was con-

nected as an enlightened agriculturist. Agriculture had been improved, but his keen insight
led him to perceive that the housing of the agricultural labourer—that most important factor
in English agriculture—had been neglected,
and he thereupon set to work to build good
and healthy cottages, but at the same time he
built farm homesteads of which we are still
proud.   Drainage too formed one of his special
studies, and turnip farming under his auspices
became an important branch of husbandry.

Mr. Lawes and Dr. Gilbert were at that
time engaged in their important investigations
regarding the fattening of cattle, and the
Duke not only rendered them all the personal
assistance which lay in his power, but also
freely placed at their disposal the resources of
Woburn Park Farm.   From his accession to
the title in 1839 to his death in 1861, Duke
Francis was a Governor of the Royal Agricultural Society.

His son William, the eighth Duke, spared no
effort to carry on the system initiated by his
father, but was precluded by illness from active
personal inspection of his estates, a work which

he entrusted to his cousin and successor, Mr.
Hastings Russell, afterwards ninth Duke of
Bedford. The latter showed equal zeal with
Duke Francis in improving the surroundings of
the agricultural labourer, and having secured
their material comfort, devoted himself to their
mental advancement. Beautiful schoolhouses
testify to Duke Hastings' predominant idea.
He, like so many of his predecessors, was President of the Royal Agricultural Society, and
founded and endowed the Woburn Experimental Farm in 1877. The ninth Duke took
the keenest interest in all branches of estate
management as well as of agriculture, and paid
especial attention to silage experiments. His
park at Woburn was described by an expert as
' the most evenly grazed and best kept,' and
the late Dr. Voelcker spoke of him as 'possessed
of the best knowledge of the details of farming
of any nobleman in the country.'

One who knew him well—Professor Jowett,
Master of Balliol—wrote :

' He built a great many churches and
schools, certainly not from the motive which
is said to have impelled great men of old to the

performance of such works. He liked to do for others what they were unable to do for themselves : to try, for example, experiments in agriculture which were beyond the means of ordinary persons. Yet he never valued himself on his good deeds, but would rather apologise for them. Sometimes when he gave hundreds and thousands he would assume the character of the receiver rather than of the conferrer of a favour. He was often believed, and sometimes believed himself, to be a pessimist ; but his pessimism or cynicism was not inconsistent with the most careful fulfilment of his duties to others. In him these qualities never obscured the fine discrimination, the just allowance, the kindly sympathy, the intense compassion for *les misérables*, which in his best moments, when he was quite sure of being understood, he gave proof of in word and deed.'

CHAPTER II

THORNEY

THE great Bedford Level, which comprises upwards of 300,000 acres and extends into six counties, with its principal area in Cambridge-shire, is the largest tract of fenland in the kingdom. It is divided by the farmers into two parts—the marshland and the fenland. By marshlands are meant low tracts gained from the sea, either by the gradual silting up of estuaries, or by embankments artificially raised for the double purpose of encouraging reclamation by the process of warping, and of protecting from the sea the lands enclosed· within them. By fenland is meant land rich in alluvial deposit, reclaimed from its former state of moor and morass by drainage, by protection from the sea by means of banks, and by the embankment of its rivers.

On the maps the great level of the Fens

looks like an enlargement of the Wash; in reality it more closely resembles a sea of land lying between the Wash and the irregular coast-line which seems to be formed round it by highlands in Norfolk, Suffolk, Cambridge, Hunts, Northampton, and Lincoln. According to historians, this Fen country has for centuries been the scene of drainage operations on a more or less extended scale. The whole surface of the basin of the Fens in which the Thorney Estate is situated is lower than the sea, the level varying from nine to twelve feet below high-water mark in the German Ocean. The difficulty of draining this tract was increased by the circumstance that the ground is highest near the shore, and falls inland towards the foot of the slope. Spongy peat, which has a natural tendency to retain water, is the material of which this inland and lowest tract consists, although of recent years on the higher parts the peaty soil is by degrees disappearing and the clay subsoil becoming more exposed. The rivers and streams, which originally found their way into the shallow estuary of the Wash, are now

caught at their point of entrance upon the
Fens, confined within the limits of strongly
constructed banks, and thus guided straight
towards the sea; the highlands, where they
immediately abut upon the fenlands, being
skirted by catch-water drains as a protection
against undue flooding. Restrained from in-
undating the low grounds, the momentum of
the body of water descending from the hills
assists in scouring out the silt from the
narrow channel in which it is confined. The
tidal waters are at the same time excluded
by sea and river banks, the latter of which
are provided at intervals, varying with the
surrounding requirements, with sluice doors
by which the flood waters escape at ebb tide.
This briefly is a description of the general
principle on which the Fen country has been
drained.

The history of the Fens is somewhat
obscure. Some authorities think that the
Romans for strategic purposes built causeways
in order to command the movements of the
Fen-men. As in Greek mythology the hero
reclaimed swamps, so in English tradition John

of Gaunt and Margaret, Duchess of Richmond,
are both credited with the work of reclamation. Be this as it may, all authorities are
agreed that the Fen country had been
reclaimed from the sea long before the days
of the Bedford Level. Thus Elstobb ('History
of the Bedford Level') states that there is
evidence ' that the greatest part of this
uncertain trackt was antiently and originally
sound and certain land naturally productive of
trees, shrubs, and bushes such as grow upon
firm and dry ground and cannot be raised nor
brought to maturity on a rotten, moorish and
morassy soil such as the Fens in general have
been for some time past.'

Lord Chancellor Bathurst (1771 *circa*) in
a judgment says: 'About three centuries
after the Conquest the Isle of Ely was one
of the most fertile countries in England until
the floods broke in, but when this occurred
antiquaries differ.'

Sir W. Dugdale (1772) quotes the description given by William of Malmesbury, who
died about 1140 :

' Thorney, though last mentioned and less

in circuit, hath the priority in fame; represented a very Paradise for that in pleasure
and delight it resembleth Heaven itself, the
very marshes abounding with trees[1] whose
length without knots do emulate the stars.
The plain there is as level as the sea which
with the flourishing of grass allureth the eye,
and so smooth that there is nothing to hinder
him that runs through it. Neither is there
any waste place in it; for in some parts
thereof are apple trees, in other vines which
either spread upon the ground or are raised up
with poles. A mutual strife there is between
nature and art, so that what the one produceth
not, the other supplies. What shall I say of
the beautiful buildings which 'tis so wonderful
to see the ground amidst these Fens to bear?'

At the beginning of the seventeenth
century the drainage of the Fens was again of
importance. The drainage works of the
Romans had been maintained and carried on
by the monks of Thorney, Crowland, Ramsey,
Ely, and Spinney, and Bishop Morton, whose
name still lives in Morton's Leam, had intro-

[1] Probably fir.

duced straight cuts and artificial rivers, ' productive in after times of the most fearful consequences.' [2]   But by the end of the sixteenth century they had fallen out of repair, and land, which previously was remarkable for its fertility, was once more submerged.   In 1635, at Skirbeck Sluice, near Boston, a smith's forge and tools were found buried under sixteen feet of deposit.   The district is naturally drained by the Ouse, the Witham, the Welland, and the Nene.   It was only on the maps that these rivers ran into the sea at the time when Francis, fourth Earl of Bedford, began to devote his attention, capital, and reputation to the task of recovering the land to its original

[2] Cf. Tennyson, *Ode to Memory* :

' The trenched waters ran
from sky to sky.'

It is the old story known to engineers that water loves its own way. The new channels, cut through porous soil, were constantly choked, and the embankments, made with material quite unsuited for the purpose, collapsed, causing great and grievous losses to life and property. The last drowning of the Fens took place in 1770, and the country lay under six feet of water. Even now there is a haunting dread of a ' drowning,' and it requires all the vigilance of that steady and unostentatious company of gentlemen known as the North Level Commissioners to prevent a repetition of that great calamity.

purpose of growing corn.   The river beds were
foul;   the   channels   choked;   the   streams
continually   overflowed   their   banks;   twice a
day the tides drove back the fresh water and
prevented the discharge of the upland streams.
The country which Francis Earl of Bedford
took in hand in the year 1630, in company
with thirteen gentlemen adventurers, had thus
become one vast deep fen, 'affording little
benefit to the realm, other than fish and fowl,
and overmuch harbour to a rude and almost
barbarous sort of lazy and beggarly people.'

The Earl of Bedford's enterprise was not
the first of its kind.   The reclamation of the
Fens had long possessed a fascination for the
keener spirits of England.   But all previous
efforts had been fitful, partial, or confined to
schemes which were never executed.   We read
of 'sessions of sewers,' surveys and commissions, and King James I. was heard to say that
'for the succour of his kingdom he would not
any longer suffer those countries to be abandoned to the will of the waters nor let them
lie waste and unprofitable; and pleased to de-
clare himself personal undertaker, and was to

have 120,000 acres as were intended to be set out for the aforesaid undertakers.'

'But something prevented him.' This is characteristic of King James I.

Then in 1629 a session of sewers imposed a drainage tax of six shillings per acre; 'but no part of this tax was ever paid.' In 1630 another session met, with the famous Dutchman Sir Cornelius Vermuyden at their elbow. ' But the country not approving of him as being a foreigner, and not liking to contract with aliens, they intimated their dislike to the Commissioners and became suitors to Francis, then Earl of Bedford, who was owner of 20,000 acres round Thorney and Whittlesea of this fenny level, to undertake the work, at whose request as also of the Commissioners he condescended thereto.'

With this application and consent the real work began. In three years the whole level was declared to be drained. Within this space of time the Earl of Bedford and his participants had spent no less than 100,000*l*., equal perhaps to 300,000*l*. at present. All the participants were completely ruined, and the Earl's circum-

stances were much reduced.   He was forced
to sell many valuable estates, not only to pay
his own liabilities, but to make good the
deficiencies of his associates.

It was an age of intrigue, and Sir Cornelius
Vermuyden had friends at Court.[3]   It was
found by courtier commissioners that in the
winter the country was under water, and
though the Fens had probably never been
more than summer lands, the Earl's undertaking was pronounced defective, and the
King was declared 'undertaker,' and was not
only to have the 95,000 acres set out for the
Earl of Bedford, but also 57,000 acres more
from the country.   'Being prevented, however,
by troubles arising in the kingdom,' the King,
it seems, did nothing in the work of draining.

In 1641 'the Civil War not only hindered
any further prosecution of these purposes,
but occasioned the works made both by him,
the said Earl, and his Majesty to decay and
become useless.'

[3] Mr. Secretary Windebank among the number. It is suggested that the action of the Court in this matter was bitterly resented by Oliver Cromwell—'Lord of the Fens.'

In 1649 ' William Earl of Bedford, son and heir to Francis, the deceased, was declared to be undertaker, and was to have 95,000 acres for perfecting thereof.' Dividing the Fens into three distinct levels—North, Middle, and South—he accomplished the work in five years.

Earl Francis no doubt suffered for employing the foreigner Vermuyden, who inundated the country with foreign labour. The drainage work was, moreover, very unpopular with the Fen-men. Earl William, unlike his predecessor, resided at Thorney in order to superintend the work, and from 1663 to 1685 devoted his energies to the often ungrateful task of reclamation. Disappointments befel him ; friends deserted the undertaking ; and he was forced not only to make advances to the participants, but to find whatever money was required for the drainage operations.

I cannot find what Earl William received for his strenuous undertaking. Dugdale mentions the fact that Earl Francis was owner of 20,000 acres around Thorney before reclamation ; but I can discover no evidence in

Dugdale, Elstobb, or Wells which shows what share of the stipulated 95,000 acres Earl William received.

If ever there was an estate to which collectivist ideas regarding land are not applicable, it is Thorney. Only 300 [4] acres of

[4] In the authorities the area is always given as 300 acres; but in Warner's *History of Thorney Abbey* a document is quoted endorsed in the handwriting of Elizabeth's illustrious minister Cecil, 'Thorney, Sir William Russell':

'A particular of the late dissolved Monastery of Thorney Abbey in the County of Cambridge with a survey of the same.

'The site where the said monastery stood contains a dwelling house of stone, in length 60 feet, in breadth 20 feet, covered with slate, and seated towards the midst of the whole lands, upon a fair drain extending east and west, whereupon also is remaining the body of the church without roof, and half of the steeple standing, with certain other decayed parts, walls and vaults of the said church and monastery, and of divers other edifices about the same, of freestone and others, to the value of 200*l.*, together with 240 acres of upland ground, whereof 160 acres is wood, 1,000 pretty oaks worth 500*l.*; the rest very good pasture, well fenced with ancient quickset hedges with some wood and timber worth 100*l.* and the land worth 6*s.* 8*d.* per acre.

'It containeth more of pasture grounds elsewhere and in divers parts lying, 360 acres of like value and goodness. So in all 600 acres worth by year 200*l.* It containeth 16,000 acres of fen grounds dispersely grown with sedge, fother, reed, willow and alder woods of five years' growth, worth 200*l.*; the grounds worth 6*d.* per acre, in all, by year 600*l.*, which in memory having been dry and firm lye now surrounded (for the most part) in water, by reason of the drains. Ever sithence uncast, and other the culturable land came to the House of Bedford on the dissolution of the monasteries. The remainder of the lordship was won from the sea and the swamps by patriotic enterprise, hard work, and lavish expenditure.

The dreary toil of reclamation had been ill requited by the Stuart Kings. Earl Francis was sent to the Tower by King Charles I., and no doubt stood a good chance of losing all his estates. His son Earl William, in the Civil War, incurred the enmity of the Parliament, and for a time his estates were sequestrated.

infinite watercourses suffered to grow up. Yet in summer, except very seldom, they are dry of themselves, and at all times and in all places men may go and beasts feed upon them.

'The whole convent lying entirely together within itself containeth by common estima- tion five miles square, which were 17,760 acres. It is en- vironed and severed on the east with several waters of its own called Gold dyke, and Knartree dyke; on the west with the water called Singlesole and Catswater, bending from Crowland to Peterborow; on the north with the river of Dowsdale bending from Crow- land to Wysbeche; and on the south with the several waters of Thorney-leame and planted in a most rich, fruitful and tradeable place to most special places of sea and land, and is and would be made for fish and fowl, besides other chief commodities, the whole several rare things of England [*sic*]. The total value of woods and stone 1,000*l*. The yearly value of the uplands and fens 600*l*.'

In the reign of King Charles II. his troubles culminated in the loss of his son William Lord Russell, beheaded for high treason in 1683. His attainder might [5] have brought dire consequences to the family, but the advent of William of Orange and the final defeat of James's hopes by the victory of Admiral Russell at La Hogue retrieved the fortunes of his race. The bill of attainder was reversed, and the father was created first Duke of Bedford. There is not much of special interest attaching to Thorney since the days of its reclamation. Quiet progress and improvement [6] form the

---

[5] 'Whether the attainder of Lord Russell would, if unreversed, have prevented his son from succeeding to the earldom of Bedford is a difficult question. The old Earl collected the opinions of the greatest lawyers of the age, which may still be seen among the archives at Woburn. It is remarkable that one of these opinions is signed by Pemberton, who had presided at the trial. This circumstance seems to prove that the family did not impute to him any injustice or cruelty; and in truth he had behaved as well as any judge, before the Revolution, ever behaved on a similar occasion.'—Macaulay's *History of England*, vol. iii. chap. xiv. Longman's edition, 1855.

[6] The *Cambridge Chronicle* of May 23, 1834, notes: 'The cost of the Nene Outfall has been about 200,000*l.*, and that of the North Level Drainage about 150,000*l.* The Duke of Bedford has been the great promoter of both the undertakings.'

chief incidents of that secluded corner, but a brief allusion may be made to the Walloon settlers of the seventeenth century. Sturdy men, who had suffered greatly for their belief, who were at first ill received in England, and who asked pathetically for man's right—employment—they proved fit agents for the patient labour which Earl Francis undertook. Descendants of the Walloons, or French-speaking Hollanders from Picardy and North Flanders, still survive. They had their own church and their own French minister, and, as late as 1727, a French baptismal register was kept. They were expert in the cultivation of corn and colza, from which they extracted oil, and there is little doubt that French influence has left its mark on Thorney agriculture. They were a quiet, industrious people, though a gravestone in the abbey churchyard tells us of one of the Le Conte family who was an exception to the rule—William Livard, *alias* Count (died 1733) :

> Here lies the unaccountable Count,
> Who died in his prime,
> Drunk most of his time.
> Rest the unaccountable Count.

Long ago the French element merged in the English ; but the Egars and the Provosts still recall the old days of persecution. And after the persecution in France there came accessions in the shape of Scotch and French prisoners, some of whom settled in the Thorney lordship.

In the days of the Stuarts there was not much security of tenure to encourage the employment of capital in the reclamation of Thorney Fen. But even in those days of civil war and revolution there probably was more encouragement for the investment of money in land than there is now. The statement may seem exaggerated ; yet the following figures will show that it is well founded.

In the period 1816–95 the taxation of Thorney has amounted to the sum of 614,714*l*., and in addition the Dukes of Bedford have expended 983,640*l*. on soil which was reclaimed by an ancestor from the inroads of the sea at the cost of 100,000*l*. The taxation paid for eighty years has amounted to nine-tenths of the net income, and in 1895 8,568*l*. was paid in general taxation, leaving a net deficit of

441*l.* on the year's working. Whatever may
have been the drawbacks to the investment of
capital in land when the Stuarts reigned, I
think it is capable of proof that modern fiscal
legislation has scarcely encouraged the spirit
of enterprise ; nor has it deepened the sense
of security in the sanctity of private property.
Low prices, bad seasons, and a crushing weight
of taxation have entirely caused rent, as understood by the political economist, to disappear
from the Thorney Estate. At the same time
the average net income for the past twenty
years, even without taking the death duties
into account, is only equal to 2¼ per cent.
interest on the capital outlay on new works.

It is sometimes urged that the pleasures
and dignities [7] attached to the ownership of a
large estate counterbalance the financial loss
and anxieties of management, and, as I have
elsewhere remarked, the critic is always ready

[7] Among these may be mentioned that the owner of
Thorney was Abbot thereof,
that he had the right of holding
market on Thursdays, and
that he held a Court of Pie
Powder. This Court of Pie
Powder was a practical institution for the summary settle-
ment of disputes at market
between buyer and seller immediately upon the spot.

with the argument that an estate, managed on commercial principles, will not involve loss. I can safely affirm of the Thorney Estate what I cannot so safely affirm of the property in Beds and Bucks, that, in a broad sense, it has been and is managed on commercial principles, with this exception—that the commercial instinct would have suggested the abandonment of Thorney in despair in 1880, and would have severed the ties which have bound my family to the old Walloon settlers of the seventeenth century.

As to the pleasures to be derived from the ownership of an estate like Thorney, if the reader conjures up a beautiful mansion and park with endless game preserves he is mistaken. They do not exist. The only pleasure which I and my forebears can have derived from Thorney is the kindly feeling [8] which has existed between us and our tenants and the inhabitants of Thorney town. It was no doubt a pleasure to my predecessors to evolve a pretty village out of the dreary waste of fens,

---

[8] As an instance, I may mention that there has never been an eviction of a farm tenant.

to create a charming river with well-wooded
banks, and to make life less malarious and less
miserable by a complete fresh water, drainage,
and sewage system, the latter worked by
steam. They have their reward in the excellence of the health of Thorney, in the practical
disappearance of crime, and in the extinction
of pauperism. In a sense these results may
be regarded as commercial; it is certain that
they are, morally, materially, and socially,
valuable results. But the economic critic is
right in his retort that such results do not
show a pecuniary profit.

A study of the Thorney Estate, and a walk
round the sea walls when the north-east wind is
rising, would, I think, convince the unprejudiced
that the theory of the unearned increment is
here inapplicable. Mill, in ridiculing the
sacredness of property, says, 'No man made the
land,' and he differentiates land from other
forms of property by the remark that it is
no hardship to anyone to be excluded from
what others have produced. Landlords, says
Mill, 'grow richer, as it were, in their sleep
without working, risking, or economising.' As

I write,[9] I am thinking anxiously of a rumour
to the effect that the storm of last week had
injured one of the sea walls, and in the next
chapter I shall endeavour to show that landlords are not necessarily growing richer in
their sleep; and I believe that most of us do
work, do run great risks, and, thanks to recent
legislation, are obliged to economise.

I also venture to think that my predecessors did make the land of Thorney. The
expenditure of 100,000*l.*[1] was no doubt a
speculation, and subsequent expenditure was
also a speculation with the ever-present risk
of 'drowning'; but why should a man,
because he is a landlord, be denied the fruits
of his enterprise and risk? There have been
other giants besides Mill. Malthus supported Adam Smith in the simple proposition 'that the interest of the landholder is
closely connected with that of the State.'
But Mill will have none of the accursed
thing. He does not like any exception to
his rules. He pronounces judgment on a

[9] January 26, 1897.
[1] Cf. *Governing Families,*   where the amount is stated
at 123,000*l.*

question which puzzles most of us—and
certainly perplexes the tenant at rent day—
in the following words: 'What is paid for
the use of farm buildings and house can no
more be called rent of land than a payment
for cattle would be. The buildings, like the
cattle, are not land, but capital regularly
consumed and reproduced, and all payments
made in consideration for them are properly
interest.' And in the same breath—perhaps
with a qualm at the thought that possibly
there was a 'means of distinguishing' in the
case of Thorney 'between an increase owing
solely to the general circumstances of society
and one which was the effect of skill and expenditure on the part of the proprietor'—Mill
cuts us off from all hope with the words: 'I
cannot think that the incomes of those who
own the Bedford Level ought to be called
profit and not rent, because those lands would
have been worth next to nothing unless capital
had been expended on them.' 'The owners
are not capitalists, but landlords.'

There is no escape from this Protean philosopher. Coming to more recent times, I am

looked upon by Mr. Marshall[2] in his clear treatise as a 'sleeping partner,' and am told that one of the fundamental attributes of land is, that it has no 'cost of production.' All I can say is that Thorney land cost a great deal to produce, and I shall elsewhere give figures as to the cost of bringing neglected farms into condition, which will suggest that not only in the initial stage of reclamation but also in the mere conditioning of a farm there is a cost— and a heavy cost of production.

[2] *Principles of Economics.*

CHAPTER III

FINANCIAL RESULTS

BEFORE entering into details, which may con-
fuse the main issue, I will at once state the
net result to myself of inheriting and owning
these estates.

The returns from the Beds and Bucks and
the Thorney properties, printed in the Appendix, show the following financial results. On
Thorney the expenditure from 1816 to 1895
amounted to 1,598,353*l.*, and on Woburn from
1816 to 1895 it was 2,632,186*l.* After spend-
ing nearly four and a quarter millions sterling
since 1816 on some 51,643 acres of land, a large
proportion of which is some of the best wheat
land in England, and after excluding all expenditure on Woburn Abbey, its park and
farm, it will be seen that at the present time
an annual loss of more than 7,000*l.* a year is
entailed on their owner. Of the sum laid out.

on the properties by the Dukes of Bedford there was spent on new works and permanent improvements :

    Thorney, 1816–1895 . . . 265,155*l*.

    Woburn, 1816–1895 . . . 537,347*l*.

The average net income derived from Thorney during the past twenty years is only 2¼ per cent. interest on the capital outlay for new works. From Woburn the return on the capital outlay for the same period, and calculated in a similar manner, amounts to barely 1 per cent.

It may not be superfluous to point out that, of the three classes interested in this agricultural estate, the owner is thus the principal loser by the mere fact of responsible possession. It is his duty to find the capital required for the construction and maintenance of buildings, houses, and cottages, and the money necessary for the development and improvement of the estate. The moment a system of management which is the creation of constant attention and of continuous owner-ship is allowed to lapse, the estate begins rapidly to deteriorate, and cannot be restored

without a costly effort.   In order to give some
idea of the many claims made upon a great
estate, the analysis of the revenue and expenditure during four typical years given on
the following pages will be of interest.

I also give a similar return for the Beds
and Bucks Estates.

The explanatory footnotes to the Thorney
statement apply equally to both returns.

Anyone who will examine these figures,
or better still the eighty years' figures printed
in the Appendix, will find it difficult to re-
sist the conclusion that Imperial and Local
Authorities have both contributed towards
the lamentable financial results.   To destroy
a system of land tenure under which great
estates are possible, may be good or bad
policy, according to the excellence of the new
system by which it is to be replaced.   If, however, the great estates are proved to diffuse
wealth, and to retard rural emigration to the
towns, it seems hardly judicious for statesmen
to crush them under the burden of a taxation
imposed at an epoch when protection and
high prices prevailed.   Still more hardly does

FINANCIAL RESULTS

THORNEY ESTATE
Extracts from Return 1861 to 1895

	Acreage	Receipts			Payments							Net Income
		Rents received	Other Receipts [1]	Total Receipts	Taxation [2]	Repairs and Maintenance	New Works and Permanent Improvements	Other Expenditure [3] including Management	Churches and Schools, including Works	Pensions, Compassionate Allowances, Charities, and other General Payments	Total Payments	
	acres	£	£	£	£	£	£	£	£	£	£	£
1846	18,604	26,125	784	26,909	5,584	3,820	3,790	2,122	335	10	15,611	11,298
1878	19,306	37,922	822	38,744	10,251	4,969	5,207	5,155	783	1,128	27,493	11,251
1879	19,307	20,515	1,319	21,834	10,457	3,442	4,255	2,484	1,057	1,838	24,083	Deficit 2,249
1895	19,369	20,186	2,009	22,195	8,568	4,825	2,744	4,575	978	946	22,636	Deficit 441

[1] These headings explain themselves. Under 'other receipts' we find items such as tolls on roads and navigation channels; receipts for grazing on the high embanked roads, locally known as droves; water rates; receipts for gravel and sand.

[2] Under the head 'taxation' come the following items: Land tax, property tax, tithe, quit, and other rents, rates, drainage taxes, insurance. Tithe, quit rents, and insurance are grouped under this head for convenience, but they scarcely affect the total as the following figures will show. Take 1879, total £10,457. Tithe accounts for £116; quit and other rents, £96; insurance, 16s.

[3] 'Other expenditure' includes such items as salaries, office expenses, audit dinners, salary of the sexton and apparitor. 'Allowances to tenants' is a frequently recurring item.

BEDS AND BUCKS ESTATES

Extracts from Return 1846 to 1895

	Acreage			Receipts				Payments								Net Income
	Estate	Woods and Plantations	Total	Rents Received	Woods and Plantations	Other Receipts	Total Receipts	Taxation	Repairs and Maintenance	New Works and Permanent Improvements	Other Expenditure including Management	Woods and Plantations	Churches and Schools including Works	Pensions, Compassionate Allowances, Charities, and other General Payments	Total Payments	
	acres	acres	acres	£	£	£	£	£	£	£	£	£	£	£	£	£ £
1846	—	— —	32,835	35,408	26,446	832	62,686	7,276	8,432	12,477	1,971	5,646	392	1,581	37,775	24,911[1]
1878	32,842	4,289	37,181	52,397	6,819	307	59,523	7,908	7,258	8,158	8,816	3,219	5,846	3,008	39,197	20,326
1879	32,860	4,287	37,147	29,882	4,869	476	35,227	8,209	6,009	7,949	10,714	2,954	8,312	8,167	47,404	Deficit 12,177
1895	28,274	4,000	32,274	23,848	5,395	2,882	32,120	6,297	7,075	4,458	7,352	4,694	2,747	5,687	38,850	Deficit 6,730

[1] Includes an abnormal receipt of £13,571 by sale of timber for railway purposes.

the imposition of the new death duties bear
on the great estates, not so much because the
losses now involved in ownership are increased,
but because the effect must inevitably tell
upon the poorer classes, in whose name, and
for whose advantage, those duties were said
to be imposed. 'Rest assured,' said Mr.
John Morley, with admirable point, 'rest
assured that taxation, however spread, however disguised, falls eventually on the shoulders
of the industrial classes.' That is to say, a
tax on land falls sooner or later on the labouring classes. It is clear that, if an estate has
to pay a large sum for several years to the
Chancellor of the Exchequer in death duties,
the money must come out of the pockets of
of those who depend on the estate. In short,
until the debt is discharged, the wants of the
farmers and labourers must be disregarded,
and the difference between 10s. 6d. and half-a
sovereign insisted upon; and it is the man at
the bottom of the ladder who is the hardest
hit by this state of affairs.[1]　Mr. Morley,

[1] A draughty cottage, a smoky chimney, a defective kitchen range, will make the home of a labourer's family

philosopher as he is, might have added that taxation or legislation, however disguised, rarely does benefit those for whom it is devised. Take for instance the enfranchisement of leaseholds. Leaseholds may be enfranchised and existing landlords may be swept away, but in their place we shall have, not the ideal and happy freeholder, but a network of capitalist companies. Go where we will, and do what we will, change everything, and capital will take advantage of the change.

As far as I can calculate, under the Finance Act of 1894, the death duties on the Thorney Estate would be 25,000*l*. Thorney yields no income, and so far as my own personal experience for two years ending 1895 extends, it has given an annual deficit. I have heard it said that, if landlords had only a small share of commercial shrewdness, they would easily be able to manage their estates at a profit. Be that as it may, and suppose

---

miserable; but where is the money to be found for repairs when there is a heavy debt to the State, which is not slow to charge a smart interest on unpaid amounts? Then, again, how is an impoverished successor to find money to pay pensions to the old and helpless labourers?

my successor has by some chance a share
of commercial shrewdness, to what use could
he put it in the case of his Thorney
inheritance ?   This would be the state of the
matter.   He must pay 25,000*l.* in order to
inherit an estate that does not pay its own
way, but is a source of perpetual expense.   He
would fare worse still in Bedfordshire, for there
he would have to pay some 40,000*l.* for a
property which left me in 1895 with a deficit
of 6,730*l.*

Under the Finance Act of 1894, my
successor could, I believe, instead of paying
65,000*l.* for an inheritance which is a source of
annual deficit, sell the estates, paying duty
upon the amount realised by the sale.   I am
told on excellent authority that the Thorney
Estate, and a good part of the Beds and
Bucks Estates, are at present practically
unsaleable ; but in the event of a forced sale,
under conditions such as I have described, no
doubt some speculators would buy, tempted
by low prices and the hope of making something out of their bargain—that something to
be realised at the expense of those resident on

the estates.   But my impression is that the
people resident on the estates would not be
greatly benefited by such a transaction, and
that they would have small cause to end their
days in praising the Budget of 1894.

Speaking at Rhymney on October 6, 1896,
Sir William Harcourt is reported in the
' Times ' to have said of balance-sheets which
show that the farmer has had no interest on
his capital nor profit on his farm :

' How comes this ?   Why, the landowner
and the farmer are partners in the cultivation
of the soil, and if there is loss, the loss ought
to be pretty fairly shared.'

Sir William went on to say :

' There is another part of the report which
gives the rents which are actually paid by the
farmers on a number of great estates.   I will
give you a few figures, and take the rent
actually paid by the tenant and not the net
income of the landlord, because on every
estate there is a variation of .the outgoings
which may take place upon it.   In dealing
with the question of the condition of the
farmer the really important question is :—

What is the farmer to pay before he can gain
any profit at all? Well now, these figures
have been given voluntarily by some of the
greatest landlords, and I will say the best
landlords, in the country, who are not men
likely to over-rent their estates. I have got
here the Bective Estate, 22,400 acres, rent
20,650*l*; a Yorkshire estate, 28,200 acres, rent
31,800*l*. ; a Cheshire estate, 16,000 acres, rent
32,000*l*. ; the Duke of Westminster's Cheshire
Estate, 14,300 acres, rent 23,700*l*. ; the Earl of
Ancaster's estate in Lincolnshire—said to be
one of the most distressed districts—46,600
acres, rent 59,400*l*. ; the Duke of Bedford—
one of the best landlords in England—(three
estates), 73,000 acres, rent 94,700*l*. ; the Duke
of Devonshire—another admirable landlord—
(four estates), 36,000 acres, rent 35,700*l*. ; the
Duke of Richmond, 12,000 acres, rent 14,000*l*. ;
These work out at an average of 25*s*. an acre,
and that is contrasted with the second part,
which shows that farmers—I do not say
farmers on these estates, but a schedule of
farmers—have received no interest on capital
and no profit on the farms. Well, it is

quite true that the rents on these estates are lower by something under 20 per cent. than they were, but I want to know whether the profits of the farmers have not fallen more than 20 per cent. If the farmer gets nothing, as these schedules seem to show, then it is plain that the whole of the net produce after the cost of cultivation goes in the form of rent.'

In referring to the Bedford Estates as yielding a rental of 94,700l., I have no complaint to prefer against Sir William Harcourt, as he was probably unaware that he was speaking of an obsolete return (1892),[2] and that the figures included house property as well as the purely agricultural returns. It may, however, be said that nothing can be more characteristic of the spirit with which Radical states-

---

[2] The figures mentioned by Sir William Harcourt as the area and rental of the Bedford Estates viz.: 73,000 acres and 94,700l. rental, are a compilation from the Blue Book of the Commission on Agriculture, entitled ' Particulars of Expenditure and Outgoings on certain Estates,' &c., &c. In supplying the Agricultural Return asked for by the Government, the figures for town property were inadvertently included. While the mistake, therefore—so far as these figures are concerned— was made by those responsible for the return, it is none the less a mistake requiring correction.

F

men allow themselves to deal with the Land Question, when the great estates are brought to the bar of public opinion, than the process by which Sir William Harcourt deduced from the figures quoted by him a rental of 25*s.* per acre over the properties which he mentions. The only way in which his result was attained was by suppressing all mention of necessary outgoings, such as expenditure on repairs and other works of maintenance.

Sir William Harcourt's point is, What money does the tenant part with annually to his landlord? If the tenant's rent is returned by the landlord to help maintain the farm, Sir William Harcourt does not mind. The tenant has had to part with money to his landlord, and, even though that money is put back again into the tenant's farm by the landlord, still the tenant has been asked to pay. This is hardly a fair view of the existence of a rent.

The present average rent per acre of farms only is as follows:

	s.	*d.*	
Beds and Bucks	16	3	per acre
Thorney and Wansford . . .	20	6	„ „
Devon and Dorset	17	0	„ „
And on the whole, collectively .	18	0	„ „

and the nominal farm rentals and the amounts actually received in 1895 were as follows :

	Nominal Rental			Actual Receipt		
	£.	s.	d.	£.	s.	d.
Beds and Bucks .	29,065	0	9	16,131	3	8
Thorney	26,196	0	0	17,567	17	6

The farm tenants would doubtless be willing to consider themselves partners with the owner, so long as they had only losses to share. But, assuming the recurrence of a period of inflated prices, and consequent large profits, the tenants would consider that the justice of the case had been fully met by the payment of their rents. The tenants are masters of the position. If prices fall, rents must again be reduced.

So far as the Bedfordshire and Bucks Estates are concerned, the reduced rental is not now sufficient to meet the necessary outgoings.

The estate, *per se*, is insolvent in point of income and expenditure, and there is no *net* rent which can reach my pocket. This insolvency, however, is due in a measure to expenditure on charities, and to the maintenance of a system in the interests of tenants and labourers which, perhaps, cannot be justly described as commercial.

Sir W. Harcourt says that rents are 'lower by something under 20 per cent.' If he had in his mind a comparison between 1878 and 1895, he would have been nearer the mark had he said over 40 per cent.

	Area in 1892	Rent received in 1892
Thorney and Wansford .	22,845	£27,963
Beds and Bucks	25,401	82,841
Devon and Dorset . . .	24,792	34,408
Totals	73,038	£94,712

While the area remains practically the same, the corresponding figures for rent received in 1895 were as follows :

Thorney and Wansford . . .	£23,080
Beds and Bucks	23,843
Devon and Dorset	82,673
	£79,596

being a reduction of the receipts of 1892 of 15,116*l.*, due entirely to decrease in rental value of farms.

It has already been stated that the foregoing amounts of 94,712*l.* and 79,596*l.*, being rents received in 1892 and 1895 respectively, represent the rental income of the whole of the landed estates, not of farms only, and are swollen by the inclusion of town property.

It may be urged that the loss entailed on landlords by reductions of rents has been already, to some extent, met by legislative relief. The Agricultural Rating Bill, for example, is cited by Radicals as a shower of gold for landowners.

It is impossible at present to estimate the relief which will be given to these estates. But it is possible to say that the relief will go entirely into the pockets of the tenants in Thorney and Beds and Bucks. There have been several relettings this year since the Agricultural Rating Bill was passed; but there has been no suggestion of raising the recently reduced rentals so as to secure to the landlord the benefits of the Bill.[3]

While I attribute much of the broken, bankrupt condition of landlords to the action of our Imperial masters, who have worried land as though its very presence was a grievance, I cannot say that our local authorities add

[3] Relief will also be given to cottagers who pay their own rates and have gardens of over ¼ acre.

much to the amenities of succeeding to an
estate.   I succeeded to the ownership of many
cottages, to which I shall allude elsewhere,
and it is my ambition that they should be
comfortable, healthy dwellings, and provided
with good gardens. Some of them were
built many years ago, in the days when
pigstyes and pit privies were fashionable.
These cottages, with their three bedrooms and
good water supply, were looked upon by my
predecessors as rather an enterprising undertaking.   But pride must have a fall, and the
Sanitary Authority determined that he would
bring my complacency down a peg. He therefore decreed that the old-fashioned privies
should be converted into the hygienic earth-
closet.   A few years rolled by, and the Sanitary
Authority said : 'You must move these pigstyes and abolish the earth-closets. A sewer is
the thing.'   So I set to work and turned the
pigstyes into tool-houses, built new pigstyes,
in a field across the road, and converted the
hygienic earth-closets into what the Sanitary
Authority knows as pan-closets.

I am always being 'moved on' by the

Sanitary Authority, always haunted with a notice to 'abate some nuisance.'

Incidentally I may mention that the energetic and suggestive Authority caused me to spend 741*l.*, or three years' gross rental of the cottages. On another block of cottages in the same place I was obliged to spend 391*l.* on similar suggestions, equal to three years' rental, and on a third block 123*l.*, or one and a quarter year's rental. I have no desire to grumble, nor to cast any reflection on the Sanitary Authority, who is one of the best of our masters. I only wish that he would universally show the same activity as he has shown on my property. I am always ready to support his action, and I sincerely hope that his efforts to obtain a high level of sanitation may be attended with success. I merely publish the facts to illustrate the occasional incompatibility between the administration of Acts of Parliament by local authorities and the profitable management of a large landed estate.

Let me give another illustration of the same point. I have established near Woburn an experimental fruit farm. An ordinary arable field was converted, during the autumn and winter of 1894, into a fruit garden by the employment of capital and labour. The land was duly planted with a valuable stock of fruit trees and bushes, and after a few months there came up—I confess to my amazement, for I had not foreseen this result of my experiment—the Overseer. Now the Parish Overseer said :—' The employment of capital has wrought a great change in this spot, and it is my duty to report the same and treble your rates.' Well, I was in search of experience in the matter of fruit farming, and I am now in a position to record an important result, it is this : If you invest capital in a fruit farm, your rates will be trebled before you have any chance of a return for your outlay.

The sequel to this incident is worth noting. In May I publicly mentioned at Thorney the trebling of the rates, and the press widely commented upon the hardship of the situation. I had been advised that it was useless to appeal against the assessment as the authority had no choice in the matter. If the property

was improved in value, the assessment must
be correspondingly increased.   Nevertheless I
appealed, with the result that the assessment
was reduced to half the amount originally
imposed.   Hence it must appear that the
pressure of public opinion brought to bear in
this case might be conveniently applied over a
larger area and on a greater scale.

I think that this method of dealing with
improvements would compare unfavourably
with the methods adopted in other countries.
Even in India improvements are protected
against enhanced taxation for lengthy periods.
If a man sinks a well in order to irrigate his
fields and to render his crop secure, the State
does not pounce down on him as the Overseer
did on me, but allows him for thirty years to
pay taxation assessed on his fields as they
were before the well was sunk.   Again, if land
is broken up from forest and brought under
the plough, it remains untaxed sometimes for
periods extending to thirty years.   Every
effort is made by the Indian Government to
attract capital to the land and to encourage
improvements.   My experience in the fruit

farm rather suggests that this is not the case in England.

In connection with the assessment of taxes let me add that, although I receive no income from Thorney or from the Beds and Bucks Estates, yet I am assessed as if I did so, and in Beds and Bucks, where the deficit for 1895 was 6,730*l*., I paid 538*l*. in income tax, and at Thorney, where the deficit for the same year was 441*l*., I paid 160*l*. 11*s*. 7*d*.

The reason is that the Inland Revenue takes no heed of what is done with income. If the owner chooses to spend all that he gets from an estate upon that estate, that is his affair. That may be reasonable, or even unavoidable; but it is not a direct encouragement to spend money on an estate.

Great estates may endure from generation to generation, provided always that the owner is capable and the management sound. But with the advent of a fool or a spendthrift come bankruptcy and sale:

> Though the mills of God grind slowly,
> Yet they grind exceeding small;
> Though with patience He stands waiting,
> With exactness grinds He all.

But democracy goes further. It will not wait in patience that sure and quiet process by which a fool and his money are parted. It tries to hasten the catastrophe by convincing every landlord, in a concrete and practical manner, that he is foolish to hold land. Hence it is that we have legislation which penalises the heir of an owner who has best managed his estate, by augmenting the death duties in proportion as the value of the estate has been increased by a judicious expenditure; rewards the starvation and ruin of a property by a light assessment, and reduces the capable owner below the level of him who has squandered or stunted his inheritance.

CHAPTER IV

THE PRINCIPLE OF MANAGEMENT ON THE BEDFORD ESTATES

ADAM SMITH assumes that the material wealth of a country is increased to a greater extent by capital employed in agriculture than by that which is used in any other branch of industry.[1] If this assumption be correct, the outlay of 4,230,539*l*. by the owners of the Bedford Estates in Cambridgeshire, Bedfordshire, and Buckinghamshire since 1816, which includes the sum of 1,138,894*l*. paid by them in Imperial and local taxation on agricultural land, has so far benefited the community as to justify some detailed examination of a system under which the State, the farmer, and the labourer at present absorb all, and more than all, the profit.

[1] *Wealth of Nations*, book ii. chap. v.

Reflections cast on the intellect, knowledge, and methods of administration of landed proprietors are, in the present day, generally accepted as true without study of the facts on the other side. Prejudices against the great landlords have been expressed in politics and in the press ever since great estates became a prominent feature in the economy of English country life. Mill declared that 'any very general improvement of land by the landlords is hardly compatible with a law or custom of primogeniture,'[2] and again, 'Great landlords have seldom seriously studied anything.'[3] Buckle, speaking of the same class, refers to 'the systematic bigotry of a body of men who are unhappily as formidable for their power as they are contemptible for their ignorance.'[4] Mill, Buckle, and the rest of their school continue to be quoted by modern politicians as though the justice and accuracy of their statements were established beyond dispute.

It would be easy to multiply illustrations

[2] *Political Economy*, book ii. chap. ii. p. 141, ed. 1868.
[3] *Ibid.* p. 142.
[4] *Miscellanies*, vol. i. p. 418.

of the popular belief in the idleness of owners
of great estates, their ignorance and their in-
veterate hostility to progress. It is alleged
against them that their voices have always
been lifted to oppose improvement. Radical-
ism and Socialism, whether Christian, revolu-
tionary, or State, are agreed in denouncing the
great estates and in demanding the subdivision
and distribution of the land, mainly in the interests of townsmen who can scarcely distinguish wheat from barley, and whose versatile
intelligence revolts against the tedious and
uncertain process of tillage.

If a fraction of the charges brought against
the owners of the great estates be true in sub-
stance, how comes it that they still survive ?
Since the first Reform Bill every institution
in the country has been on its trial. Those
that survive have been strengthened in the
process. No institution that does not command the respect of democracy can hope to
preserve its existence ; and, if the 'Story of a
Great Estate' does not succeed in justifying
the present system of land tenure, it will at
least show that the profits of successive owners

have not been the only, nor even the first, consideration of my predecessors.

I admit that, in some respects, the administration of the Bedford Estates has not been
conducted on strictly commercial lines.   An
admission that the Bedford system of land
management has not been carried on with gain
as the sole or principal object, will, in the eyes
of a large number of critics, carry with it self-
condemnation. Further examination, however,
will show that the system, in so far as it has
departed from the principles which govern the
successful higgling of the markets, has not
been conceived or carried out in the pecuniary
interests of the owner.   On the contrary, its
object has been to realise among the agricultural population such a standard of moral and
physical well-being as would have been unattainable by strict adherence to commercial
lines of administration.

As I have already stated, the system owes
its origin to my predecessors, and, whatever its
character, my connection with it confers on me
none of the credit due to them.   I have therefore the less scruple in describing some of the

more prominent features which are common to many of the great estates. Mr. Froude, in writing of the uses of a landed gentry, says : ' It appears to me, for the reasons that I have given, that a landed gentry of some sort must exist in a country so conditioned as ours. The only question is whether we shall be satisfied with those that we have, or whether we wish to see them displaced in favour of others, to whom the land would, or might, be a mere commercial speculation. Abolish primogeniture, compel either by the law or by the weight of opinion a subdivision of landed property, it will still be bought up and held in large quantities, but it will be held by men of business who, being no longer able to look forward to permanence of occupancy, therefore having no motive for securing the goodwill of the people living around them, will regard their possessions from a money point of view, and will aim at attaining the largest possible amount of profit and pleasure for themselves.' [5]

Referring to Francis, fourth Earl of Bedford, Mr. Froude says :—' There was no place for a

[5] Froude's *Short Studies*, vol. iii. p. 424.

Russell by the side of Laud and Strafford, and
Bedford set himself to improve his property
and drain the marshes about Whittlesea and
Thorney.   If solid work well done, if the addition of hundreds of thousands of acres to the
soil available for the support of English life, be
a title to honourable remembrances, this Earl
ranks not the lowest in the Cheneys pan-
theon.' [6]

If the fourth Earl of Bedford did good service to the State when he recovered rich lands
from the bottom of the sea, his more recent
descendants have used their inheritance with
no less regard to the occupants and tillers of
the soil thus regained.   No feature in the system
thus established by them better illustrates the
truth of this proposition than a history of the
cottage property on their estates.

I know of no more satisfactory form of
philanthropy possible for the owner of a great
estate than the provision of good cottages.
There is, moreover, nothing more important to
a landlord than the question of cottage management.   Good and comfortable cottages, in

[6] Essay on Cheneys and the House of Russell.

G

which the decencies and dignity of human life
may be maintained, generally imply that they
are inhabited by good and efficient labourers.

That the problem of housing the labouring
population on these estates has been one of
considerable importance may be seen from the
following figures :

	No. of Cottages in 1894	Population
Beds and Bucks	768	2,595
Thorney and Wansford .	423	1,653
Devon	552	2,235
Dorset	60	240
	1,803	6,723

It will be noticed that the cottages are not
over-crowded, as the ordinary calculation of
five persons to a cottage would give a population of 9,015.

The system of a weekly tenancy, which
has long been in force on these estates, is
obviously open to theoretical objections. As
a matter of fact, not only do successive
generations of cottagers continue to occupy
these dwellings, but the system works well in
the interests of the tenantry themselves.[7]

[7] This is shown by the fact that the descendants of cottagers living on these estates early in the century are now more numerous than those of farm tenants similarly descended.

Only a few weeks ago an aged cottage tenant was found to have made a will leaving her dwelling, held on a seven day tenure, to a near relation. Such hereditary tenants, provided they work on the estate, are to be encouraged, and their existence in considerable numbers is evidence of the essential soundness of the system. The hereditary cottage tenantry form a healthy nucleus of population which does not seek the glare and excitement of the towns, and a system that encourages them may fairly be said to conduce to the national welfare.

Cottage property on these estates has represented a considerable financial loss. The rents are nominal. They are neither based on the capital outlay nor calculated on the ability of the tenants to pay. The management of the cottages is a source of constant care and anxiety, and unless the cottage foreman be carefully chosen as a man of tact and good feeling, friction and discontent are inevitable. In considering the staff of a great estate, it is not easy to overrate the importance of the cottage foreman, whose reports are checked by a system of inspection by the highest executive authority on the property.

One fertile source of grievance is the removal of a decreasing family from its old home to a smaller cottage, in order to make room for a young and growing family. This, as the young people grow up and go out into the world, is a necessity of cottage management. Irritation also arises from the introduction of some new sanitary requirement which hitherto has been an unheard-of novelty. The prohibition of lodgers has also been known to produce resentment. Very often the change of garden is the source of trouble, and the loss of a favourite fruit tree occasions justifiable lamentations. In all such cases the kindly tact of the foreman is required. Upon him devolves the duty of mitigating the natural feeling of irritation which is created by necessary changes.

The general sentiment of the cottage tenantry was recently expressed by an aged and solitary widow, who was asked by the management to share a cottage with another widow, on the ground that, if living alone, she

might some day set fire to herself or her
cottage. In refusing the proposal, she said :
' I want the house to myself, and do not want
to be messed about.'

Nevertheless, when the ruthlessness of the
commercial system is frankly abandoned,
difficulties arise, which foil an energetic and
business-like management responsible for the
financial results. Many of the cottages are
inhabited by estate pensioners. I have heard
of more grumbling from the pensioners than
from all the rest of the cottage tenants put
together. It would be an easy matter to avoid
all difficulties by letting the cottages with
the farms ; but, in that case, deterioration
of the buildings and their inhabitants would
ensue, because no one would be concerned to
maintain the cottages in good order, and decay
of the dwellings is invariably followed by
degeneracy in their population.

The fullest investigations I am able to
make convince me that the condition of
cottage property is intimately associated with
the character of the inmates. If the cottages
are well built, conveniently arranged, plea-

santly situated, and of size suitable for the
various families of inhabitants, there is a
marked tendency on the part of the inmates
to live up to the standard of their dwellings.
When, on the other hand, cottages are allowed
to run to ruin, the character of the inmates
commonly deteriorates with that of their dwellings, and the contagion of their example influences their neighbours for evil.

The arrangements and design of a cottage
are matters of supreme importance. If there
are two doors to the dwelling, there is a tendency, amounting in some cases to a practice,
to leave one unused. It is found also that, if
two dwelling-rooms of the same size are
provided, one is often kept idle as a parlour,
where china dogs, crochet antimacassars, and
unused tea-services are maintained in fusty
seclusion. This idle parlour adds nothing to
the comfort of the cottagers. The best plan
is to divide the ground floor into one good
living-room, one kitchen, one back kitchen or
scullery, and one spacious and airy pantry.
There is a growing inclination on the part of
the rural population to avoid single cottages

as being lonely and cold.   For a pair of
cottages a joint washhouse is sufficient; but a
partition wall dividing the court is desirable.
Cottages should be built in pairs or fours, if
the tastes and interests of their inmates are
consulted.   When new cottages are built at a
distance from a village, it is always wise to
contemplate the possibility of the building
becoming one day the dwelling-place on a
small holding.   As regards the garden, a con-
sensus of opinion among real cottage gardeners
decides that one rood clear is as much as one
man in regular work can manage successfully.
Cottage gardening without a pig is never
wholly satisfactory, and the pig consequently
receives every encouragement on the Bedford
Estates.

The sanitary arrangements of the cottages
have passed through a continuous and costly
process of evolution.   While it cannot be said
that perfection has yet been reached, there is
a marked contrast between the arrangements
to-day and those that prevailed in the days
when scientific sanitation was unknown.   The
theory of the dry earth system is excellent;

but, as is the case with other good things, it is
too often merely a theory.   In wet weather
dry earth is unattainable.   On the whole, the
pail system is satisfactory, if the garden is large
enough to render trenching unobjectionable.

Another feature in cottage property, closely
affecting the comfort and health of the people,
is the pantry or larder.   Until recently this
essential convenience was disregarded, and,
in this respect, there is a good deal of lee-way
to make up.   The washhouse, too, is a matter
of importance.   In Thorney, and elsewhere,
the washhouse is sometimes placed inside the
cottage, and is used not only for laundry purposes, but also for boiling pigs' food.   Discomfort and ill-health are the results of this error of
arrangement, and the process of expelling the
washhouse from the cottage to the barn is being gradually carried out.   It is possible that
the old bakehouses may be utilised as wash-
houses.   In many of the older barns a relic of
the days of dear bread is found in the shape of
a bakehouse for 'the joint use of neighbours.
The bakehouse is a thing of the past.   In England bread is almost universally procured from

the baker, and I find that, in some parts, even
the Scot no longer cooks oatmeal, but buys
white bread from the travelling baker's van,
and, in consequence, Scottish children are
rapidly deteriorating. It would be very expensive to give each cottage a new washhouse,
and the only drawback to the common use
of laundry accommodation is the tendency to
quarrel. This, however, is a lesser evil than
washing in the house, especially if, as sometimes happens, a smoky chimney increases the
disadvantage and misery of life. A smoky
chimney or a kitchen range that does not
work is enough to condemn any cottage ; but
the architects and surveyors who can invariably avoid these evils have yet to be found.
There is something pathetic in the gratitude
expressed by many of the cottagers when
discussing the improvement in their lives
caused by a new chimney-top or blower.

One of the chief drawbacks to cottage life
is the discomfort caused by draughts. When
there are two doors, wind, wet, and cold enter
freely, and, in addition to the through draught,
the draught down the open chimney is con-

sidered a great drawback.   To my mind, every
cottage should have a porch with a porch
door.   No room, saving the third or boys' bedroom, should be built without a fireplace, both
on account of ventilation and in case of illness.
The boys' bedroom should have a ventilating
shaft connected with the chimney, and the
family should be induced to keep the shaft
open.   Though I advocate fireplaces in the
other two bedrooms, I am well aware that in
practice they are rarely used, and that the
occupants often seek to exclude ventilation by
blocking up the chimney.   The general need
for thorough internal whitewashing is met on
the Bedford Estate by the management.

The question of the pigstyes was always
cropping up until their provision by the estate
was finally resolved on.   The objections to the
landlord providing pigstyes are obvious.   The
cost is enormous.   The work tends to drag on
for years.   There is no certainty that the pigstyes will be used.   On the other hand, that
part of the English system of landownership
which consists of the landlord providing all
necessary buildings, if not followed in the case

of the pigstyes, is apt to create difficulties on a change of tenancy. The pig and the garden plot are interdependent, and no cottager who is without a pig can be said to be making the best of his opportunities.

The County Councils give instruction in cooking, and most useful that teaching is, provided the women are able to take proper advantage of it. The kitchen ranges supplied to the cottages, however, have occasionally interfered with the beneficent educational designs of the Local Authority. Arrangements are now made for securing for the future uniformity of efficiency in the kitchen ranges, a virtue which cannot always be attributed to them in the past.

From what has gone before, it will be seen that the cottage management and cottage inspection call for special qualities in those responsible for them. As the men to whom these difficult and delicate duties are entrusted grow old, serious difficulties will arise if no system is established to train younger men in their places. Personal knowledge of the different families is essential, and this knowledge cannot be improvised or rapidly acquired. A system of understudies to the chief foremen is indispensable.

In the main, cottages must be regarded as part of the essential equipment of the land—treated agriculturally—and should be under the direct control of the landowner.

The commercial view of the situation is perhaps best illustrated by such examples as cottages annexed to collieries, slate-quarries, railways, factories.

The generally accepted view is that it is the duty as well as the wisdom of the landowner to house the labour necessary for his estate. If the owner fails in his duties in this respect, he will quickly see dilapidated and insanitary dwellings, inhabited by a wild and even dissolute population, planted at his door.

The financial intimacy of the relations between homestead and cottage is clearly shown by the (at one time) almost universal practice of letting the cottages with the farms, just as coastguard cottages must be reserved for coastguard men, or barracks for soldiers. This is still very much the practice. It is fol-

lowed on the Crown estates, and its adoption
has indisputably saved an immense amount of
trouble in management. 'I let you this farm
with its three cottages for a term of years, on
condition that you insure, pay tithe, land tax,
and all rates and taxes, and do all repairs,
rough timber being provided for you out of my
woods and hedgerows.' Such a system of
management practically leaves little for the
steward to do beyond the half-yearly collection of the rents. It suggests no financial
loss to the owner in respect of cottages specifically, any more than of barns and stables or
cow-sheds specifically, but is expressed as a
whole in farm rent, reduced of course in correspondence with the obligations thus accepted
by the tenant. Yet such a system is attended
with grave defects.

This method of dealing with cottages was
formerly practised on the Bedford Estates.
But gradually other considerations have come
into play, such as public health legislation,
building byelaws, sanitary rates, overcrowding,
neglect of repairs. The advantages of local-
ising labour, instead of permitting it to be

removed to a distance of perhaps a couple of
miles, were more clearly seen : the substitution
of yearly tenancies for leases shifted the responsibility from the tenant to the landlord,
for no yearly tenant will substantially repair.
From these and other causes cottages have
come to be direct holdings, a return for which
is partly expressed in cottage rent and partly
in the rent of the farm.

The change, simple as it may seem, but
absolutely unavoidable, has added largely to
office work and to the duties and responsibilities of the steward. On the other hand, it
has proved, I believe, of immense advantage
both to the estate and the community, and,
notwithstanding some irritation, which always
attends rules and supervision, to the cottage
tenants especially. At the same time that
this great change has had to be faced, it has
become in these times more than ever necessary that cottage management should be conducted on sensible business lines.

The figures given below for 1895 are offered
in illustration of the foregoing remarks, and in
proof of the serious aspect which the cottage

question necessarily wears for the owner of the land :

ESTATE COTTAGES IN 1895

	Beds and Bucks Estates		Thorney Estate	
Number . .		768		817
Area . . .		131 acres		82 acres
Income . .		£2,780		£1,390
Expenditure—	£		£	
Taxation .	386		177	
Management	372		150	
Repairs . .	2,646		1,146	
Works . .	375		1,571	
Sundries .	10		—	
		3,789		3,044
Deficit .		£1,059		£1,654

the deficit being at the rate of 27*s.* per cottage in Beds and Bucks, and upwards of 5*l.* per cottage in Thorney.

It is thus seen that, taking an average of four individuals per cottage (a low estimate), the Beds and Bucks Estates house a population of some 3,000, and the Thorney Estate one of 1,300, at an absolute cash loss to their owner, the rental being more than absorbed by the expenditure for taxation and maintenance, which on these estates is paid by the landlord.

It is interesting to note the occupation
of these cottages, as shown by the following
table :

	Beds and Bucks	Thorney
Occupied by effective labour . .	517	269
Occupied by non-effective labour—		
Widows and spinsters . . .	92	22
Pensioners	24	—
Tradesmen or higglers . . .	42	13
Persons not employed by me or		
my tenants . . .	77	2
Persons unable to work . .	16	11
Total non-effective labour . .	—— 251	—— 48

The result of these figures is to show that
the percentage of non-effective labour housed
in the cottages is—

Beds and Bucks   .   . 32 per cent.
Thorney,   .   . 15 ,,

A fair estimate of the cost of these cottages,
exclusive of the value of their sites and gardens,
shows a capital outlay of—

Beds and Bucks   .   . £114,000
Thorney   .   .   . 57,000
                   £171,000

Had this large outlay been invested in Consols
it would have been producing an income of

some 5,000*l.* a year; invested in cottages it
produces nothing, rental being absorbed by
necessary expenditure.

It must, however, be borne in mind that, as
the cottages are a necessity for the labour of
the farms, they have a value apart from rental,
because without them the land would, under
present conditions, be unletable.

The table on page 99 shows the financial
results of cottage building on various parts of
the Beds and Bucks Estates.

GARDENS

Passing from the occupation of these
cottages to the gardens attached to them, we
find on the Thorney Estate that the extent of
gardens let with cottages and their rent are
as follows :

There are 210 cottages in Thorney having
gardens included in the cottage letting, the
total area of which is 68 acres 3 roods 29 poles,
or an average of 52¾ poles to each cottage.
The rent is merged in that of the cottage, but
where gardens have been recently enlarged, an

H

extra rent of from 4*d.* to 5*d.* per pole has been charged. The necessary fencing, however, is included in this charge, which, for anything less than one acre, almost invariably costs the fee simple value of the land itself. The remaining cottages on the estate are situated in the town; but, as the gardens are not immediately attached to them, but are let separately as garden allotments, they have not been included in the foregoing statement.

BEDS AND BUCKS ESTATES

Comparison of Rent received from various Cottages on average of five years, ending 1895, with original Outlay upon Buildings

No. of Cottages in Block	Cost per Cottage	Original outlay in building	Situation of Cottages	Average Rent received for five years	Average Outgoings				Net Receipts	Percentage on outlay
					Taxation	Management	Repairs	Total		
	£	£		£ s. d.	£ s. d.	£ s. d.	£ s. d.	£ s. d.	£ s. d.	
No. 5	185	674	Woburn: Bedford Street, Nos. 23 to 27; built in 1850–1851	18 6 3	3 19 5	2 1 4	6 11 10	12 12 7	5 13 8	1
20	158	3,155	Millbrook: Nos. 12 to 31 (Sand Hill Close) built 1858–1863	68 18 0	12 0 6	7 15 9	39 0 7	58 16 10	10 1 8	0·3
2	314	628	Ridgmount: Nos. 67 and 68 (Brogboro Middle Farm) built 1871–1872	8 2 0	19 6	18 3	6 3 10	8 1 7	5	Nil
2	753	1,507	Willington: Nos. 49 and 50 (Hill Farm) built 1879–1880	7 12 8	12 6	17 3	5 19 6	7 9 3	3 5	Nil
2	327	653	Milton Bryan: Nos. 1 and 2 (Fountaines Farm) built 1882–1883	8 4 8	16 6	18 8	6 6 9	8 1 11	2 9	Nil
31	213	6,617		111 4 1	18 8 5	12 11 3	64 2 6	95 2 2	16 1 11	0·24

The figures for ' Taxation ' and ' Management' are apportioned, not *actual*; but they are very near the mark.

CHAPTER V

CHARITIES

No survey of the system followed on these estates would be complete which did not include detailed reference to the voluntary payments to churches and schools, and the provision of pensions and charitable gifts to labourers and other persons resident or employed on the estates. I give a return for forty years of the payments made under this heading in respect of the Beds and Bucks Estates. The net income of the estates for the same period is also given, and, for convenience of reference, nine years of deficit are. also tabulated.

From these figures it will be observed that during the nine years in which a deficit occurred, there was no diminution of expenditure on churches, schools, or estate pensions.

BEDS AND BUCKS ESTATES

Statement of Voluntary Payments to Churches and Schools,
Pensions and Charitable Gifts from 1856 to 1895

Year	Churches and Schools	Estate Pensions and Allowances	Gifts and Charities	Totals	Net Income
	£	£	£	£	£
1856	2,045	815	575	3,435	7,124
1857	1,140	741	551	2,432	16,511
1858	1,901	692	733	3,326	15,017
1859	1,127	670	693	2,490	12,735
1860	1,209	646	586	2,441	10,442
1861	640	1,139	752	2,531	13,054
1862	745	472	695	1,912	9,666
1863	498	472	306	1,276	14,163
1864	3,177	546	760	4,483	14,751
1865	8,465	579	884	9,928	5,617
1866	11,761	572	546	12,879	3,854
1867	15,853	573	609	17,035	Deficit } 7,531
1868	23,281	680	628	24,589	Deficit } 14,520
1869	8,897	693	651	10,241	7,854
1870	4,968	1,724	873	7,565	12,434
1871	4,855	1,899	931	7,685	10,783
1872	5,958	2,110	3,006	11,074	11,484
1873	3,967	2,079	1,237	7,283	17,008
1874	3,746	2,062	1,314	7,122	21,568
1875	3,903	2,029	1,623	7,555	13,338
1876	3,735	1,550	1,545	6,830	11,915
1877	11,480	857	1,545	13,882	10,903
1878	6,203	864	3,824	10,891	20,326
1879	8,437	1,009	2,118	11,564	Deficit } 12,177
1880	5,828	1,355	2,025	9,208	Deficit } 5,241
1881	2,282	1,251	1,281	4,814	8,528
1882	1,428	1,158	944	3,530	15,252
1883	2,521	1,125	830	4,476	15,668
1884	1,987	1,370	1,303	4,660	8,270
1885	4,404	1,328	913	6,645	Deficit } 701

STATEMENT OF VOLUNTARY PAYMENTS, &c. (*continued*)

Year	Churches and Schools	Estate Pensions and Allowances	Gifts and Charities	Totals	Net Income
	£	£	£	£	£
1886	7,036	1,306	643	8,985	7,057
1887	8,267	1,358	1,989	11,614	Deficit 3,575 }
1888	2,492	1,453	504	4,449	7,455
1889	3,060	1,583	1,681	6,324	10,955
1890	2,694	1,457	2,652	6,803	10,464
1891	2,699	1,773	552	5,024	10,468
1892	3,461	1,777	1,130	6,368	6,365
1893	1,204	1,964	985	4,243	Deficit 798 }
1894	2,401	2,391	1,080	5,872	Deficit 9,732 }
1895	2,941	2,442	1,076	6,459	Deficit 6,730 }
Total	£192,786	£50,564	£46,573	£289,923	£300,024

NINE YEARS OF DEFICIT

Year	Deficit	Charities
	£	£
1867	7,531	17,035
1868	14,520	24,589
1879	12 177	11,564
1880	5,241	9,208
1885	701	6,645
1887	3,575	11,614
1893	798	4,243
1894	9,732	5,872
1895	6,730	6,459
	£61,005	£97,229

It is obvious from a glance at these figures that, if the estate had been strictly speaking managed upon a commercial basis, a surplus might have been realised by the simple process of dropping the charities during the nine lean years. The nine deficits amounted in the aggregate to 61,005*l*., while the sum of the charities distributed in those years exceeded that sum by 36,224*l*.

Again, it will appear from the foregoing return that for forty years the average *annual* expenditure on charities amounted to 7,248*l*., whereas in the years of deficit the voluntary payments, so far from being curtailed, reached the larger average of 10,803*l*., thus illustrating the distinction between the commercial system warmly advocated by modern land reformers, and that followed on the Bedford Estates.

The cost of maintaining schools on the estates prior to the Education Act of 1870 might fairly have been included under the head of charities. I have, however, refrained from thus treating the outlay on those objects, since, although there was no legal obligation on the part of landlords to educate the children of the labourers, the social obligation to do so was accepted as one of the conditions of ownership, and in this spirit was discharged as a matter of duty. When the Whigs threw in their lot with the late Mr. Forster's policy, those of them who were landowners were taunted with being actuated by motives of personal advantage, as the public provision of education was held to relieve the pockets of the proprietors of the great estates. In whatever light the maintenance of schools prior to 1870 may be regarded, all expenditure on that object after that date is charitable in essence, since there has been neither legal nor social obligation to supplement the School Board system. That system came into force in the time of the ninth Duke. He held that the minds of children were greatly affected by their physical environment, and he sought to give them bright and healthy surroundings in their homes and schoolrooms. I see from the accounts that in Bedfordshire one school cost 5,268*l.*, and another 6,013*l.*, but it was money well laid out. Duke Hastings

was a strong supporter of the Board-school
system. He made twenty-four school-houses
over to the authorities at a nominal rent of
10s. per annum each, and the estate still keeps
those houses in repair. During his time
16,307l. was spent on schools in Beds and
Bucks, and 2,657l. in Thorney. It is a
matter of congratulation that the bitter and
deplorable strife aroused by the question
of dogma has never invaded our parishes.
Duke Hastings' readiness to spend money in
building schoolhouses, remodelling old schools
and equipping them with the newest appli-
ances, did not, however, prevent the school rate
from rising above Mr. Forster's sanguine 3d.
Thus, in the parish where the school was
built for 6,013l., the school rate is 7d.; while
in the other parish mentioned, where a sum
of 5,268l. was expended, the rate is now 1s.
In another parish where he assisted by
additions and alterations, the rate stands at
1s. 5d. But school rates seem to have a
compensating influence, for, in the first
instance quoted, the rates in 1869 and the
rates at the present time are exactly the same;

in the second instance the rates are lower
now by 3*d*. than they were in 1869. The moral
seems to be that the more the country spends
on education the less it will have to pay in
other directions.

It is very difficult to give exact figures as
to the amount which the Board-school system
costs the estate, but the recent establishment
of a new Board school synchronising with a
revaluation of rent enables me to give an
account. The school building will cost me
2,800*l*., and as a set-off to the school rate,
56*l*. 0*s*. 6*d*. has been taken off the farm rents.

It may be added that since 1870 the rule
never departed from is to decline all assistance
to voluntary schools.

Finally, it may be pointed out that while
the net income for forty years averages 7,500*l*.
per annum, the average annual outlay on
charity amounts to 7,248*l*. These charities
may perhaps be advantageous to the State by
preventing rural depopulation, to the tenantry
by attaching the labourer to the land, and
to the labouring classes by giving them an
honourable refuge in their old age. Further,

they may, it is hoped, add to the sum of human happiness. But they can neither be defended on commercial principles, nor are they likely to be repeated under any future and alternative system of land tenure that may be adopted.

A similar return for Thorney is given on page 109 for the period 1870–95.

No detailed analysis of these figures is required, as the system is identical with that followed on the Beds and Bucks Estates. This will be seen by comparing income and charitable outlay during the years of deficit.

Some details regarding the provision for the old age of persons employed on the two estates may be given here. The list is not comprehensive, but typical pensions are quoted.

ESTATE PENSIONS

(1) BEDS AND BUCKS ESTATES

Estate pensions range from 2s. per week (5l. 4s. 0d. per annum) to labourers' widows, to 266l. per annum to a former chief clerk,

and those now subsisting may be classed as
follows :

			£	s.	£	s.
2 clerks	{ 1 at £266 per annum 1 „ 25 „ „ }		291	0		
1 gardener	„ 80 „ „		80	0		
1 bailiff	„ 80 „ „		80	0		
1 dairyman	„ 31 4s. „ „		31	4		
1 dairywoman	„ 44 4s. „ „		44	4		
3 foremen	{ 2 „ 12s. week or £31 4s. each per annum 1 „ 10s. week = £26 per annum }		88	8		
1 watcher at 15s. week = £39 per annum			39	0		
1 lodgekeeper at 14s. 6d. week = £37 14s. per annum			37	14	691	10

32 labourers, &c., viz. :			
1 at 12s. week = £31 4s. per annum	31	4	
9 „ 10s. „ = £26 each „ „	234	0	
9 „ 8s. „ = £20 16s. „ „	187	4	
4 „ 7s. „ = £18 4s. „ „	72	16	
7 „ 6s. „ = £15 12s. „ „	109	4	
1 „ 5s. „ = £13 „ „	13	0	
1 „ 4s. „ = £10 8s. „ „	10	8	657 16

9 widows, viz. :			
1 of bailiff = £50 per annum . . .	50	0	
1 of labourer at 6s. week = £15 12s. per annum	15	12	
1 of labourer = £18 per annum . .	18	0	
4 of labourers at 2s. 6d. week = £6 10s. each per annum	26	0	
2 of labourers at 2s. week = £5 4s. per annum	10	8	120 0

£1469 6

THORNEY ESTATE

Statement of Voluntary Payments to Churches and Schools,
Pensions and Charitable Gifts from 1870 to 1895

Year	Voluntary Payments to Churches and Schools	Estate Pensions and Allowances	Gifts and Charities	Totals	Net Income
	£	£	£	£	£
1870	1,393	1,043	121	2,557	13,766
1871	1,576	1,006	168	2,750	13,518
1872	1,411	759	1,144	3,314	14,201
1873	1,360	583	208	2,151	15,867
1874	1,352	537	183	2,072	11,747
1875	1,133	603	256	1,992	2,797
1876	945	711	300	1,956	584
1877	925	684	92	1,701	5,199
1878	783	555	273	1,611	11,251
1879	1,657	512	378	2,547	Deficit } 2,249
1880	2,099	438	843	3,380	1,476
1881	1,035	454	716	2,205	Deficit } 4,579
1882	726	507	730	1,963	15,955
1883	1,875	470	140	2,485	10,847
1884	884	449	276	1,609	11,958
1885	833	487	185	1,505	2,112
1886	668	656	179	1,503	10,096
1887	682	646	539	1,867	Deficit } 815
1888	3,361	447	50	3,858	12,407
1889	1,181	495	175	1,851	8,380
1890	844	499	161	1,504	8,134
1891	666	455	93	1,214	13,843
1892	722	456	88	1,266	3,130
1893	950	363	90	1,403	3,538
1894	932	225	255	1,412	Deficit } 1,815
1895	978	199	92	1,269	Deficit } 441
Total	£30,971	£14,239	£7,735	£52,945	£180,907

(2) Thorney Estate

Estate pensions now subsisting are as follows :

	£.	s.
1 widow of a former tenant, £40 per annum . . .	40	0
1 widow of a workman, £15 12s. per annum . . .	15	12
1 retired schoolmistress, £10 per annum . . .	10	0
2 estate foremen—1 at £80 and 1 at £50 per annum .	130	0
1 carpenter at 8s. per week = £20 16s. per annum .	20	16
3 labourers at 5s. each per week = £13 per annum .	39	0
	£255	8

I think it can be argued that not only the weekly allowance, but also the cheap cottage have a most important influence in keeping men off the rates. Looking at the list of Thorney men now actually in Peterborough Workhouse, only one can be regarded as being remotely connected with the Bedford Estates, and none of them have ever been employed by the estate. Few parishes of a purely agricultural population of nearly two thousand souls can boast of such freedom from pauperism.

A further consideration presents itself in

connection with the 'uncommercial management' of the Thorney and Beds and Bucks Estates.   Drunkenness and crime are practically non-existent at Thorney.   Commercial management would smile at the abolition of a paying public-house, or the erection of a reading-room, yet this uncommercial policy saves the rates and the State from the creation and maintenance of paupers and criminals.

Weekly allowances and yearly pensions should, if possible, be kept separate.   Weekly allowances to labourers are in the nature of old age pensions.   They cannot be justified from a commercial point of view; but, inasmuch as a weekly allowance keeps a man from the workhouse, the system assists the State and saves the ratepayer.   While the system, therefore, aims at no agricultural Utopia, it does, at all events in some measure, fulfil the objects dear to social reformers, who desire to establish a national plan for saving the workers from the poor-house as their only asylum in old age.   The great provident societies succeed in encouraging thrift among a portion of the town populations, but inhabitants of the rural districts have difficulty in learning the thrift that prepares for a rainy day.

CHAPTER VI

RENT REMISSIONS AND REVALUATIONS

ON the Bedford Estates, disastrous seasons, foreign competition, and other causes set forth in detail by a succession of Royal Commissions, have required either revaluations or the re-adjustment of rents on no less than seventeen occasions since 1879. Much is alleged by land reformers as to the artificial character of rent remissions in England. It is urged, with some show of reason, that rent remissions in this country express nothing more than the operation of an inflexible natural law, by which owners, determined to exact the uttermost farthing for their land, are obliged to make concessions to their tenants, who would throw up their farms unless adequate consideration were extended to them in their difficulties. The matter of remissions, however, is by no

I

means so simple as it may appear on the surface. Many elements enter into the problem of what is a fair rent, besides the more obvious reasons for lowering the hire of land and buildings which appeal to the land reforming confraternity. Prior to 1879, there is no trace on these estates of general remissions of rent, though a reduction took place on the Thorney estates from 1822 to 1827. From 1879 to 1895 the remissions averaged 26 per cent. per annum, and in 1881 and 1895 revaluations were made which resulted in a general reduction, equal to about 10 and 35 per cent. respectively, on the rents previously paid. The effect of these reductions has been to reduce the interest received during the last twenty years on the capital invested in buildings and improvements in Beds and Bucks to less than 1 per cent., and in Thorney to less than 2 per cent.

Previous to 1879, with the exception named, rents seem to have increased on relettings. In some few instances the advance was due to outlay by the owner for improvements made at the request of the tenants.

The remissions of rent to the tenants of Thorney since 1879 have been as follows :

1879	50 per cent. of the year's rents.			
1880	25	,,	,,	,,
1881	25	,,	,,	,,
1882	25	,,	,,	,,
1885	50	,,	,,	,,
1886	12½	,,	,,	,,
1887	50	,,	,,	. ,,
1888	10	,,	,,	,,
1889	16⅔	,,	,,	,,
1890	25	,,	,,	,,
1891	12½	,,	,,	,,
1892	32½	,,	,,	,,
1893	37½	,,	,,	,,
1894	50	,,	,,	,,
1895	25	,,	,,	,,

(50 per cent. off half-year to Lady Day, 1895.)

The rental, as will be seen, showed a steady growth up to 1878, when it attained its maximum figure of 35,525l. for Thorney and 43,975l. for Beds and Bucks.

The cycle of bad seasons, which commenced in 1875, culminated (as was then supposed) in 1879, when the difficulties of that most disastrous year were met with a remission to all farm tenants of half a year's rent.

A continuance of untoward weather, coupled with diseases in cattle and rot in sheep, was accompanied by a steady fall in the value of produce; and in 1881 the Thorney farms were revalued, with the result of reducing the rents by an average of nearly 10 per cent.

The continuous fall in prices called for repeated help in the shape of remissions (as stated in the return) until 1895, when, on the advice of experts, rents were once more adjusted to the times by an all-round reduction of 35 per cent.

The general statement of expenditure and receipts, which is printed in the Appendix, shows that, although the revaluation of Mr. W. C. Little in 1895 gave a decrease of 35 per cent., the total remission in that year is equal to 42½ per cent.

The following extracts from the steward's annual reports as to the remissions of rents on Thorney will illustrate and explain the reasons for which they were made :

1879. *Remission of rents.* — In consequence of the repeated wet seasons, and the general depression in agriculture, there was remitted to the tenants of all farms and accommodation fields on the Thorney Estate a receipt for the half-year's rent due at Lady Day, 1879.   The tenants expressed their gratitude by presenting an address.

The total remitted and repaid was 17,976*l*. 8*s*. 5*d*.

1880. In consequence of the repeated wet seasons and the general depression in agriculture, there was remitted to the tenants of all farms, other than those who had given or received notice to quit, a sum equal to 25 per cent. of the year's rent due at Lady Day, 1880.

The total was 8,165*l*. 16*s*. 1*d*.

In spite of this liberal concession, following that of 50 per cent. in the previous year, sixteen of the tenants were either partially or wholly in arrear on December 31, 1880, for the half-year's rent September 29, their due arrears amounting in the aggregate to 2,814*l*. 13*s*.

1881. The Lady Day audit of 1881 was collected with much difficulty, but without a general remission.

That of Michaelmas, 1881, was, in consequence of the continuous wet, postponed till March, 1882, when a remission of 50 per cent. (being 25 per cent. of the year's rent) was given.

1882. The audit of Lady Day, 1882, was abated by a remission of 50 per cent. (25 per cent. of the year's rent), 'in consideration of the deficient yield of the last two harvests.'

Mr. James Martin's revaluation, which operated from Lady Day, 1882, represented a reduction of 10 per cent. on Thorney farms, as compared with 1879.

In 1883 and 1884 rents were paid in full.

1885. Owing to the deficient harvest of 1884 and the continued agricultural depression, the remission of the entire half-year's rent due at Lady Day was made.

1886. The continued depression, coupled with falling prices, was met by a remission of 25 per cent. of the half-year's rents to Lady Day (equal to 12½ per cent. of the year's rent). No remission was made from the half-year's rents to Michaelmas; but in December, 1886, a circular was addressed to all agricultural tenants, announcing that the entire half-year's rent to Lady Day, 1887, would be remitted.

1887. The half-year's rent to Lady Day was forgiven.

1888. A remission of 20 per cent. of the half-year's rent to Lady Day, 1888 (10 per cent. of annual rental), was directed in consequence of the continued depression in agriculture.

1889. For the same reason, one-third of the half-year's rent to Lady Day, 1889 ($16\frac{2}{3}$ per cent. of annual rental), was remitted.

1890. The continuous fall in prices of both stock and corn called for further help, and a remission of 50 per cent. of the half-year's rental to Lady Day, 1890 (equal to 25 per cent. of annual rental), was granted.

1891. For the same reason, 25 per cent. was remitted from the half-year's rent to Lady Day, 1891 (equal to $12\frac{1}{2}$ per cent. of annual rental).

1892. The continued depression, with ever falling prices, had now brought matters to an acute condition.

Hitherto, in spite of frequent calls for permanent reduction of rents, the difficulties of the situation had been met by recurring remissions, in the hope that the depression would pass.

It was now, however, apparent that a permanent reduction must be made, and, pending the consideration of this question, a remission of 40 per cent. (20 per cent. of annual rental) was made from the half year's rental to Lady Day, and in November, 1892, a circular was addressed to the farm tenants informing them that 25 per cent. of annual rental for three years from Lady Day, 1892, would be remitted.

This, for the half-year to Michaelmas, 1892, brought up the remission for the year to $32\frac{1}{2}$ per cent. of annual rental.

1893. In November, 1893, it was directed that, having regard to the increased difficulties, a further remission of 25 per cent. should be made, in addition to that promised for the three years current, and that this additional remission should also be made in respect of the half-year to Lady Day, 1894.

This made the remissions for 1893 equal to 37½ per cent. of annual rental.

1894. The remission of 25 per cent. in addition to that promised for the three years to Lady Day, 1895, made the total remission for this year equal to 50 per cent. of annual rental.

Owing to the continuance, and indeed the intensification, of the great depression in agriculture, the question arose of further assistance to the tenants, with the result that a permanent reduction of 35 per cent. was decided upon.

This reduction was made known to the tenants by circular, dated November 22, informing them that, for the half-year to Lady Day, 1895, they would receive a remission of 50 per cent. (25 per cent. of annual rental), and that thenceforward their rents would be reduced by 35 per cent.

1895. Remission of 50 per cent. off half-year's rental to Lady Day (equal to 25 per cent. of annual rental), as above.

The total rental of Thorney farms in 1878 was 35,525*l*. On the revaluation in 1895 it was reduced to 21,613*l.*, a reduction of 13,912*l.*, being (say) 40 per cent.

The total amount remitted at Thorney from 1879 to 1895 is 145,911*l.*

The following extracts from the steward's annual reports show the remission of rents on the Beds and Bucks estates :

1879. *Remission of half a year's rent.*— In consequence of the depression in farming, 50 per cent. of the farm and occupation rents for the year 1879 was remitted, no Lady Day audit being held.

1880. In consequence of continued depression in farming, 25 per cent. of a year's rent was remitted to all farm tenants at the Lady Day audit.

1881. At the Michaelmas rent audit in December, 1881, a remission of 25 per cent. of a year's rent was made to those tenants who had had no recent abatement made in their rents ; and to those whose abatement in rent was less than 25 per cent. the difference between their reduced rent and 25 per cent. of a whole year's rent was made good to them in the form of a remission.

1882. At the audit for the Lady Day
rents collected in June, a general remission
was allowed to farm tenants of 10 per cent.
on the revised rental, in consequence of the
sad and continued depression in agriculture.

In 1883 and 1884 rents were paid in full.

1885. The half-year's rent due at Lady
Day, 1885, was remitted at the June audit to
the whole of the farm tenants, excepting to
those who were in arrear, or who were quitting
at Michaelmas, 1885.

1886. In consideration of the continued
difficulties under which farmers were suffering
from low prices, aggravated this year by poor
crops, instructions were given at the June
audit to return farm tenants $12\frac{1}{2}$ per cent. of
the year's rent due at Lady Day. At the
December audit tenants paid in full. Subsequently it was intimated to all farm tenants
by circular that the whole of their rents due
next Lady Day would be remitted.

1887. The half-year's rent due at Lady
Day was remitted in full, as announced to the
tenants in December, 1886.

1888. A remission of 30 per cent. on the

year's rent was made to all agricultural tenants on the Beds and Bucks estates.

1889. A remission of 25 per cent. was made from the half-year's rents of farm lands at the Lady Day audit, excluding those tenants who had their farms at rents valued according to times prices.

1890. A remission of 50 per cent. was made from the half-year's rents of farm lands at the Lady Day audit upon the usual lines, which excluded those tenants whose farms had been revalued at times prices and those tenants who were in arrear.

1891. A remission of 12½ per cent. on the year's rent was made to all agricultural tenants on the Beds and Bucks estates holding at unrevised rentals.

1892. A remission of 20 per cent. on the year's rent was made to all agricultural tenants on the Beds and Bucks estates holding at unrevised rents.

The remission amounted to 4,944*l*. 11*s*. 6*d*.

Notwithstanding the above concession, nine tenants were in arrear at December 31.

1893. By circular dated February 1, 1893,

all farm tenants holding at unrevised rents were informed that 25 per cent. of rental until Lady Day, 1895, would be remitted.

And by circular dated November 1, 1893, they were told that, owing to the increased difficulties of the times, they would receive an additional remission of 25 per cent. for the half-year ending Michaelmas, 1893, and Lady Day, 1894.

By the provisions of these circulars, tenants holding at unrevised rentals received a remission of 37½ per cent. on the year.

A remission of 25 per cent. was also made to tenants holding at times prices from the half-year's rents due at Michaelmas.

The remissions amounted to 9,200*l.* 7*s.* 7*d.*

Seven tenants were in arrear at December 31.

1894. By circular dated November 22, 1894, farm tenants holding at unrevised rents were informed that, in addition to the remission of 25 per cent. promised until Lady Day, 1895, there would be a further remission of 25 per cent. from the half-year's rents due respectively at Michaelmas 1894, and Lady Day, 1895.

The remission to tenants holding at unrevised rents was thus 50 per cent., and to tenants holding at times prices 25 per cent. of the year's rental, and amounted to 13,082*l*. 0*s*. 10*d*.

One tenant only was in arrear at the end of the year.

1895. The promised remission of 50 per cent. from the Lady Day rents was supplemented by a further remission of 50 per cent. from the rents due at Michaelmas.

The farm tenants holding at unrevised rentals were, therefore, in receipt of a remission of 50 per cent., those tenants holding at times prices participating to the extent of half that amount.

The remission amounted to 13,188*l*. 13*s*. 9*d*.

There was no arrear at the end of the year.

To summarise the situation :

Total rental in Beds and Bucks in 1878 amounted to	£43,975
Total amount of rents remitted since 1879 .	132,222
The revaluation of rental made in 1895, and brought into force with effect from Michaelmas, 1895, was	20,063
Showing a reduction of	23,912
Being (say) 55 per cent.	

In spite, however, of this reduction, and in
spite of the reduction made in Thorney, remissions still materially affect the income of the
estate.

Thus, in Thorney, where the revaluation involved a reduction of rents amounting to about
40 per cent., it is still necessary in 1896 to grant
remissions to the extent of 1,422*l.* 10*s.* 4*d.*,
while in Beds and Bucks the remissions for
the same year reached the total of 1,172*l.* 15*s.*
It should be added that, in addition to the
reduction of 55 per cent. made in the rental of
the Beds and Bucks estates by the revaluation
of 1895, the landlord has relieved the tenants
of two charges. In the first place, the landlord now maintains boundary fences; in the
second place, he insures the farmhouses and
buildings, relieving the tenant of this charge.

HAPTER VII

ALLOTMENTS AND SMALL HOLDINGS

In the Allotments Extension Act of 1882 an allotment is defined as 'a small piece of land let to a person to be cultivated by him as an aid to his sustenance, but not in substitution for his labour for wages.' Sec. 13 (4) fixed the maximum allotment at one acre, a great advance on the ideas formerly prevailing.

In 1834 the Poor Law Commissioners considered that a man with a big family could not with advantage occupy more than half an acre. 'Such an amount appears to be the utmost which he can cultivate and continue to rely on his wages. If he becomes, in fact, a petty farmer before he has accumulated a capital sufficient to meet, not merely current expenses, but the casualties of that hazardous trade ; if he has to encounter the accidents of the seasons, instead of feeling them at second hand after their force has been broken on the higher classes, his ruin is almost certain.'

In the Allotments Act of 1887 the same maximum of one acre was observed—Sec. 7 (3) —and this limit was undisturbed in the Allotments Act of 1890. But under the Local Government Act of 1894, Sec. 10 (6), the parish council ' may let to one person an allotment or allotments exceeding one acre, but, if the land is hired compulsorily, not exceeding in the whole four acres of pasture, or one acre of arable and three acres of pasture.'

It has always been a point of honour with my predecessors to co-operate loyally with the Legislature in respect to measures affecting the land. Long before the Allotments Extension Act of 1882, the labourers on the Bedford Estates had their gardens, to meet the wants of which elsewhere the Allotments Act was subsequently invoked.

But although the various Allotments Acts came as no novelty to the Bedford management, they brought about a general enlargement of existing cottage gardens. The Local

K

Government Act of 1894, however, introduced a new scheme, and in pursuance of the policy of the Act, an offer was made to each parish council to take over existing allotments in the terms set forth in the correspondence which appears at the close of this chapter.

The result was not unsatisfactory, as it seemed to indicate approval of the existing system. Thirteen parish councils in Beds and Bucks were offered the chance of becoming landlords. All of them declined the offer.

We have therefore been obliged to go quietly on by ourselves. A subsequent statement will show the number of half-acre and acre allotments on the estates under review. Seeing that the Legislature regarded one acre of arable as the limit of an allotment, in some places acre allotments have been created. We have further done our best to show the labourers that no recourse need be had to 'compulsory hiring.' But here a difficulty arises. The limit of area laid down in the Local Government Act of 1894, a limit that was no doubt inserted only after full inquiries,

does not apply to voluntary lettings.   As
I desire to give every facility to labouring men
to acquire allotments I object to being forced
into 'compulsory hiring,' recognising that
the machinery of the Act must necessarily
add considerably to the rent of the allotment.
In recent cases I have endeavoured to
bring my voluntary lettings under the spirit
of the Act, by asking the various parish
councils to prepare regulations for the sanction
of the Local Government Board.   It remains
to be seen, however, whether the Local
Government Board will, in sanctioning such
regulations, insist on the limit contained in
Sec. 10 (6) of the Act of 1894, or give any
advice to parish bodies as to the essential
character of the allotment.

My own experience, as I have elsewhere
remarked, leads me to think that one quarter
of an acre as a cottage garden will tax to the
utmost the energies of a labourer in full work ;
and though I loyally accept the apparent view
of the Local Government Act, that there are
men who can toil all day for wages and yet do
justice to one acre arable and three acres of

pasture, I fear that disappointment may arise, and that loss to the ratepayers and trouble to the tenant farmers may result if the original and sounder conception of the allotment is lost sight of. A man who thoroughly culti- vates an acre of land grows more than he can consume, and must face the ' casualties of that hazardous trade,' agriculture. It is significant that village tradesmen have already begun to regard allotments as a cause of bad debts and arrears. Definite cash wages afford a surer credit than the produce of allotments. However, I have determined to give every encouragement to the provisions of the Local Government Act of 1894, though I hope that good cottage gardens will be found preferable to any allotment.

In view of the continued depopulation of rural districts, the decline of agriculture, and the effect of education in creating in the mind of the labourers a distaste for the cultivation of the land, the expediency of giving the rural population a larger interest in the soil of the country is generally admitted. It is contended by many that the allotment system, when wisely applied, is beneficial to all concerned. It benefits the labourer by adding to his daily sustenance, and by affording him a profitable occupation for his leisure : it benefits the farmer by retaining labour in the neighbourhood : and it may perhaps be said to benefit the State by counteracting the attraction exercised by the great towns over our country population. But the movement, if it is to be healthy and permanent, must be placed on a business footing. It will assuredly languish if it is regarded as a dole or charity, and in the letting of land for allotments certain facts must be borne in mind.

Plots of land, when once detached from the rest of the estate and prepared for allotments, must be cultivated either by the cottage tenantry or by the owner. Death, illness, change of residence and idle habits impose upon the landlord the necessity of continuing with hired labour the cultivation of land that is only profitable to a labourer living on the spot and working for himself in his spare time.

When the allotment system was first

introduced, an allotment was understood to be a piece of ground additional to the garden, or in lieu of a garden, upon which a farm labourer should grow such vegetables as could be consumed in his own family. The labour devoted to his allotment, however, was not to interfere with his day's work on the farm, nor was it intended that he should compete in the market with the farmer and gardener by selling produce. He and his family required fruit and vegetables, and these he could grow more cheaply than he could buy. But the Local Government Act of 1894 seems to take a wholly different view of the system. It launches the labourer on a commercial speculation, and makes him the rival of the farmer and the market gardener.

My own view is that the best possible arrangement for the labourer himself is a cottage and a sufficient garden for all family wants. Next, the allotment in lieu of the garden when garden and cottage cannot go together; but I doubt at present whether the labourer is well advised in attempting to grow for the market. At the same time, if the Act of 1894 is evidence of the wish to try 'the commercial speculation,' I would never oppose the attempt. A man cannot well ruin himself over an allotment as he can over a small holding : therefore, wherever there is a wish to try the experiment, I have always given facilities to those desirous of embarking in the venture. I think, too, that, apart from the question whether in certain soils and situations an allotment will pay, there is the further consideration that the surplus labour and energy which a man puts into his allotment is not to be measured by hard and fast rules of profit and loss. The vegetables grown on one's allotment, and the pig—that essential auxiliary—are more succulent and sustaining than the cheaper products of the market.

It is an invidious task for a parish council to pick and choose between applicants, and often men are given allotments with the sure knowledge that they will fail in this as in everything else they touch. Again, the landlord is under a great disability as regards notice to quit. The tenancy is a yearly one, terminable at Michaelmas by two months' notice. A man

who has just found other employment in an
adjoining parish has given me notice to vacate
his acre allotment, and claims compensation
for seed and labour. I have tried without
success to obtain another tenant. Meanwhile
the outgoing tenant will feel that he has a
grievance if he is held to his agreement, and
the allotment will be neglected all the summer,
with the result that it will be extremely difficult to let it next Michaelmas. These difficulties, arising from the mobile and transitory
character of the labouring population, greatly
complicate questions of cottage management
and allotments.

Of course it is a nice point whether an
owner holding the view that there is a risk in
growing for the market should be a direct party
to the speculation, or should delegate the responsible function of 'allotting' to the parish
council. Perhaps the safer policy is to give
all the cottages a rood of garden, and to lease
to parish councils an ample supply of good
land for allotting to those adventurous spirits
who want more than one rood.

The whole question is very difficult, and

there is as yet but little experience which enables us to foretell the results of the system. So far as gardens of one rood are concerned no doubt arises, and the movement is good in every way and to be encouraged. As regards allotments of one to four acres, it is better perhaps to let them through the parish councils, if indeed the latter bodies will accept the responsibility; for, as will be seen from the correspondence on the subject at the end of this chapter, there seems little hope that the parish councils will consent to accept risks and responsibilities which now fall exclusively on the owners of the land.

Allotment rents are admittedly higher than those paid by farmers, but this is due to the fact that an allotment tenant is a retail customer for choice land near his home, while the farmer is a wholesale customer for bad and good land taken together. Moreover, the owner is obliged to carve out allotments from his estate, and substitute for a compact and easily managed property a collection of patches difficult to control and costly to administer. Instead of dealing with a man of established position, equipped with capital, and possessing agricultural experience, the owner is placed in immediate relations with a varied collection of men, some of whom, from no fault of their own, are necessarily lacking in capital and experience.

In these circumstances the rent of allotments will always be higher than the rent of farms, because the labour and cost of dealing with them, and the risks involved in the transaction, are much greater than those involved in dealing with farm tenants. Applicants for an allotment, moreover, are sometimes inclined to forget that the land they wish to cultivate is already being cultivated by someone else, and that this larger customer must be displaced and compensated before the smaller, or retail, customer can be installed.

On the whole, I think that legislation regarding allotments, though it has happily been but little used, has worked beneficially in advertising the movement. The attitude of the farmer, which at first was supposed to be hostile, is now one of good-humoured tolerance.

On the other hand, the labourer, who used to trace the decadence of agriculture to the apathy and poor cultivation of the farmer, now has an opportunity of himself learning the chilling influence of prices.   Thus the legislation on the subject of allotments has perhaps established one point of common sympathy between the farmer and the labourer.

The following details as to allotments may be of interest :

ALLOTMENTS ON THE THORNEY ESTATE

		a.	r.	p.
Total area		41	1	5
		£	s.	d.
Gross rent		120	7	3
Average gross rent per acre		2	18	4
Landlord's expenditure, viz.:				
Taxation . £13 17				
Fence repairs 8 4				
		22	1	0
Expenditure per acre . .			10	8
Net rental		98	6	3
Average net rent per acre .		2	7	8

There are 212 allotments.   Of these, 41 are half-acre allotments.   The ground made over for this purpose was 21 a. 1 r. 1 p., which after deducting paths and fences shows a balance of land actually let to the allotment holders of 20 a. 2 r. 0 p. In these half-acre allotments the average rent is 1*l*. 3*s*. 9*d*.

The remaining allotments, 171 in number, represent an area of 20 a. 0 r. 4 p. of ground taken from the estate. The average size of these allotments is 17½ poles, and the average rent is 5¾*d*. per pole of ground actually let. All outgoings for rates, taxes, and repairs are borne by the landlord.

On the 41 half-acre allotments the practice is to grow wheat or barley on half the area and potatoes on the other half, the plough cultivation for the former costing about 1*l*. 6*s*. 6*d*. and for the latter about 1*l*. 7*s*. 3*d*. The following are the various methods of cultivation and their approximate cost, from which it will be gathered that spade cultivation would entail an additional expense of 7*s*. in the case of the wheat, and 8*s*. 3*d*. in that of the potato crop. It is interesting to notice that there is an excellent system of co-operation among the allotment tenants, both in cultivation sometimes, it is believed, in the purchase of manures.

¼ Acre Wheat

Plough Cultivation	s.	d.	Spade Cultivation	s.	d.
1 load manure .	3	0	1 load manure .	3	0
Ploughing . . .	2	0	Digging . . .	9	0
3 stone wheat at			3 stone wheat at		
1s.	3	0	1s.	3	0
Drilling and har-			Drilling and har-		
rowing . . .	2	0	rowing . . .	2	0
Rolling	0	6	Rolling	0	6
Hoeing	3	0	Hoeing	3	0
Reaping, &c. . .	5	0	Reaping . . .	5	0
Carting	2	0	Carting	2	0
Threshing . . .	6	0	Threshing . . .	6	0
	£1 6	6		£1 13	6

¼ Acre Potatoes

Plough Cultivation	s.	d.	Spade Cultivation	s.	d.
1 load manure .	3	0	1 load manure .	3	0
Ploughing . . .	2	6	Digging . . .	10	0
Ridging . . .	1	3	Trenching and		
Planting . . .	1	6	planting . . .	3	6
Closing ridges .	1	3	Hoeing	2	6
2 sacks potatoes			2 sacks potatoes		
at 3s. . . .	6	0	at 3s.	6	0
Moulding up . .	1	3	Moulding up . .	2	6
Digging-up crop .	8	0	Digging-up crop .	8	0
Hoeing	2	6			
	£1 7	3		£1 15	6

Recent low prices have affected the demand for allotments; had it not been so, the impetus caused by the recent legislation would have caused an increase in the number of applica-

tions; as it is, there is a very lukewarm demand
at present, and when there is an allotment
to let, it becomes a question of position
and aspect whether the applicant will take it
or not.

BEDS AND BUCKS ESTATES

	a.	r.	p.
Total area	359	2	27

	£	s.	d.
Gross rental	732	19	0
Average gross rent per acre	2	0	9

Landlord's expenditure, viz.:

	£	s.	d.
Taxation . .	£155	6	2
Fences . .	150	5	9
Small payments	13	0	
	306	4	11
Expenditure per acre . .		17	1
Net rental	426	14	1
Average net rent per acre .	1	3	8

There are 1,621 allotments. The area ap-
propriated for the purpose is 359 a. 2 r. 27 p.;
the area actually let is only 339 a. 3 r. 32 p.
The difference is accounted for by paths and
fences. The average size, including half-
acre and acre plots, is about 30 poles, and
the average rent is $3\frac{1}{4}d.$ per pole.

There are ninety-four half-acre and acre
allotments. The ground surrendered was

62 a. 1 r. 21 p. ; the ground actually let is
58 a. 3 r. 1 p.

In 1895 the allotments unoccupied were :

Parish						
— — —	. . .	5				
— — —	. . .	9				
— — —	. . .	2				
— — —	. . .	2		a.	r.	p.
— — —	. . .	1	Acreage .	2	3	28
— — —	, . .	1	Rent. . .	£6	19	6
		20				

Our figures for 1896 show that the number
of unoccupied allotments is increasing.

Previously to the year 1891, all allotments
were held by the tenants direct under written
agreements.   It was estimated that sufficient
land was laid out in each parish to provide each
labouring man who lived in an estate cottage
with an allotment of about 20 poles, or one-
eighth of an acre, but the extent of allotment
ground let to one man frequently exceeded this
amount.   It was held that a labouring man
could not with advantage occupy a greater
extent of allotment than he could cultivate
himself, or by the aid of his family.

About the year 1885, applications were

received for additional allotments and for allotments of greater extent (acre and half-acre allotments), and in 1891 the demand was first met in a Bedfordshire parish by letting to the Rural Sanitary Authority under the Allotment Act, 1887, twenty acres of land for the provision of acre and half-acre allotments.

This land was selected by the applicants as suitable, and formed part of one of the principal farms. It was part of a grass field. The land was fenced and laid out at the cost of the landlord, and handed over to the Authority on a yearly tenancy from Michaelmas, 1891, on the following terms: Rent, 2*l*. per acre (net measure); landlord to pay rates and taxes; tenants to repair fences and gates; tenants to be at liberty to break up the land from grass to arable.

The Authority at first let the land to the tenants at 44*s*. per acre, but subsequently reduced it to 42*s*., it being found that 2*s*. per acre would be sufficient to provide the Authority's expenses for management, repairs, &c.

The capital outlay incurred in rendering

this land available as allotments was as
follows :

	£	s.	d.
Tenant-right	20	0	0
Surveying and measuring	5	19	9
Fencing, gates, and road-making .	42	13	5
	68	13	2

and the effect of the transaction is as follows :

	£	s.	d.
Deduction from the rent of former occupier.	35	0	0
Annual rates, formerly paid by previous tenant	3	15	0
Interest on capital outlay of £68 13s. 2d. at 2½ per cent..	1	14	4
	40	9	4

The present rent being 40l., the estate
loses 9s. 4d. a year, and in addition incurs
the risk of losing the capital outlay, and of
finding itself with an arable instead of a pasture
field to deal with, in the event of the termina-
tion of the tenancy.

Although the land was only hired in 1891,
an application for a reduction of rent was made
at Michaelmas, 1892. This was declined, but
on a renewed application, representing the land
to have been foul on entry, half a year's rent
was returned at Lady Day, 1893.

L

In 1896 a small holding, but without house and buildings, containing

	a.	r.	p.
Pasture	1	2	34
Arable	6	2	0
Total	8	0	34

came into hand, and on application it was let to the parish council at 50s. per acre, being the same amount paid by the outgoing tenant. The parish council paid tenant-right. There were many applicants for this small occupation, and the parish council now sublets the grass field at about 6l. per acre.

Parish	No. and description of occupiers	No. of allot-ments	Acreage		
			a.	r.	p.
A	*One*, a nurseryman . . .	5	0	2	20
B	*One*, small holder and hay dealer	47	5	0	30
C	*Three*, butcher, baker and publican	15	2	1	8
D	*Two*, carter and carpenter	18	3	0	30
E	*One*, publican	26	4	2	19
F	*Four*, coal dealer, publican, ragman, carrier .	42	5	3	18
G	*One*, timber dealer . . .	18	2	0	1
H	*One* publican	7	0	3	4
	I.e. in 8 parishes 14 men hold	178	24	2	5

The foregoing table shows the number and extent of allotments at the present time in the hands of those other than labourers.

Other cases of letting to tradesmen could be found, but the above table deals with surplus land after the demands of the labouring population are satisfied.

Owing to the cost of managing single allotments—one here, and another there, and frequently wide apart—it is the practice to avoid cultivating them by the estate staff, and they are usually dealt with by letting them to a tradesman or other person willing to hire them (failing any application from a labourer), or by letting them for one year to a farmer or tradesman on a reduced rental for such a period, on the understanding that they are to be given up when applied for. When no one can be found willing to cultivate them, the rubbish is kept down by the estate staff.

It sometimes happens that a man leaves his allotment partially cultivated, and it is then compulsory that the work should be carried on for the year by the estate men until it can be relet.

SMALL HOLDINGS

Some confusion is likely to be caused by recent legislation as to the meaning of a small holding. At present our only knowledge is that allotments may extend to four acres. Between allotments and small holdings there is, I think, a wide gap. A few words on the history of a successful experiment at Thorney may not be uninteresting.

By reason of its easy working, its fertile soil, and the comparatively small amount of capital per acre necessary, the Thorney Estate is peculiarly adapted for the purpose of testing—from the point of view both of landlord and tenant—the commercial value of small holdings. In 1888 about ninety acres were set aside for the purpose of supplying small holdings to four applicants, who were chosen out of a number of labouring men, desirous of cultivating a piece of land not exceeding twenty or twenty-five acres in extent. The holdings in question were within easy reach of Thorney, and, in order to prepare them for occupation, it was necessary to erect suitable buildings, and to lay down and to fence a certain proportion of the land for grass. The tenants entered upon their new occupations in 1889. A small homestead was erected on each holding, consisting of a granary, an open yard with two bay shelter hovels, loose box, cow byre, calves' house, cart hovel, poultry house, and an outside copper. A small stackyard and six acres of grass were divided from the arable land, the total cost of these works being 640*l*. 6*s*. 8*d*. With regard to the four occupiers themselves, No. 4 was a farm hand who had served one master as foreman for many years. His capital was 190*l*. Nos. 1 and 3 were hardworking men employed on the estate, their capital at the outset being 175*l*. and 160*l*. respectively. No. 2 was a thatcher, also on the estate, his capital being 150*l*. Accepting their own statements as correct, three out of the four tenants at the beginning of 1897 were worth over 300*l*. apiece. No. 1 has not done quite so well, but has a large head of cattle and horses for so small an occupation, and gives no sign of regretting the experiment he has made.

Nos. 2 and 4 value their 'outside' labour at 10*l.* per annum, No. 3, 23*l.*, and No. 1, 35*l.* for the same period, this last sum being mainly caused through the tenant undertaking the carting of coal and road material.

Three out of these four occupations were at the outset in a foul and impoverished condition. The valuer actually awarded 57*l.* 10*s.* 7*d.* by way of cultivation dilapidations against the outgoing tenant, and in addition to this it was advised that a further consideration of 45*l.* might equitably be conceded. This was done. Since the experiment began the prices have been the worst ever known within the memory of man, and the seasons for fenlands have been only moderately favourable. Notwithstanding these facts, the rent in every case has been punctually and cheerfully paid. According to the statements of the tenants themselves, their capital has so materially increased that it seems clear that, under certain conditions, small holders can do more than hold their own, and can bear favourable comparison with the larger occupiers. The holdings in question are far from being on one of the best parts of the estate, but nevertheless, if liberally treated, are capable of producing fairly heavy crops, of which wheat and oats predominate, a sufficiency of mangolds for wintering the stock being grown, and also potatoes for home consumption. A dairy in each case is kept, calves being raised, and a large head of poultry materially aids the business. I am able to quote another instance of an industrious small occupier who, in spite of bad times and very considerable difficulties at the outset, has so improved his position as to be able to undertake the occupancy of a larger holding, into which he will enter at an early date.

The following case is interesting, as an example of a small occupier not succeeding in his efforts :

A. B. was a foreman bricklayer in the store yard at Woburn. He was discharged when the store yard was broken up in the year 1880, his wages then being 2l. 5s. per week. On leaving he received a gratuity of 117l. This, together with his savings, probably made him the possessor of about 300*l.* He desired to embark upon agriculture, and a holding containing about thirty acres was let to him from Michaelmas, 1881. Of this over sixteen acres were pasture. At that time he was able to work at his trade of bricklaying, and undertook work of this description for probably two or three days in the week, attending to his farming the remainder of the time, his wife superintending in his absence. As time went on he was unable to augment his income from farming by receipt of wages, and was also able to do less on the land himself, and resorted to hired labour. To make matters worse, prices of produce began to fall, his land became gradually worse and worse in condition, until he found himself unable to carry on any longer, and at his own request he was relieved of his occupation at Michaelmas last —the last year's rent being cancelled.

Even with these concessions it is feared that, after realising his stock-in-trade, he has little more than 50*l.* or 60*l.* left. His age is now sixty-seven. It is important to notice this contrast to the success obtained in

Thorney. It points to a fact which applies equally to allotments as to small holdings—viz. that success, apart from the ability of the occupier, depends chiefly on the soil of the holding. It is folly to lay down the proposition that allotments or small holdings are universally desirable, but it is safe to say that in certain localities and on certain soils they are most desirable and in every way to be encouraged.

The small holdings at Thorney were created at Lady Day, 1889. The initial cost of laying them out, and the area and rent and subsequent reduction of rent were as follows :

Cost of buildings, fences, and laying down to grass six acres of land &c.			Area			Rent 1889 to 1895			Present Rent		
£	s.	d.	a.	r.	p.	£	s.	d.	£	s.	d.
No. 1. 163	8	6	19	1	30	31	15	0	22	0	0
„ 2. 163	8	5	24	3	35	39	5	0	27	0	0
„ 3. 163	8	5	22	1	22	33	15	0	23	10	0
„ 4. 163	8	5	21	1	7	32	0	0	23	10	0

In 1894 four new cottages were erected on the holdings at a total cost of 999*l*. 9*s*. 10*d*.

The small holders, as regards the land in their occupation, shared in the general reduction of rents (35 per cent.) on the Thorney Estate as from Lady Day, 1895, but continue to pay the full rent of their cottages ; they were also allowed the same remissions of rent from year to year as the Thorney farm tenants in general, viz. :

1890—25 per cent.	1893—37½ per cent.
1891—12½ „	1894—50 „
1892—32½ „	1895—25 „

To sum up, it will be gathered from the foregoing remarks that to the tenants the Thorney small holdings have been an undoubted success, without causing a serious diminution in the landlord's rental income, as will be seen from the following figures.

The reduced rental of the land when formerly occupied as part of the farm out of which the small holdings were carved was 18s. 9d. per acre ; the present rent paid by the small holders is 17s. 8d. per acre. For the capital outlay of 1,653l. (which includes the cost of the new dwellings), the rent apportioned for the cottages, 4l. 15s. each per annum, or 19l. in all, represents a return of 23s. per cent., which is fully equal to the rate of interest received in respect of the cottage property generally on this estate.

It is hoped that the repairs of the four sets of small buildings will not be relatively greater than would be required for the larger buildings of one farm of the combined area, while on the other hand there are no labourers' cottages to provide and maintain, as would be necessary in the case of the larger farm.

ALLOTMENTS AND PARISH COUNCILS

The advantage of transferring the management of allotments to the parish councils having recommended itself to Parliament, a circular letter was sent to the several parish councils on the Beds and Bucks and Thorney Estates, offering to them respectively the tenancy of the allotments in their parishes.

The letter was addressed to the chairmen of twelve parish councils, and a similar offer was addressed to the chairman of an urban district council.

The offer was in each case declined, the councils refusing to undertake the risks and responsibilities involved in the transfer of the management of allotments from private to public enterprise; and the replies and resolutions in the appended correspondence show the unanimous feeling of the local governing bodies, that allotments are too speculative an investment to be indulged in by trustees of public funds.

Circular Letter

' SIR,—The Local Government Act of last Session having empowered Parish Councils to to take upon themselves the charge of allotments, I am directed to inform you that, subject to arrangements with the present tenants, His Grace is prepared in accordance with the principles of the Act to transfer to the Council over which you preside all his field allotments in ——, as per enclosed list, on a yearly tenancy on terms to be agreed between His Grace and the Parish Council, provided such should be the wish.

' The Parish Council paying rates and taxes (except land tax, landlord's property tax, and tithe and rates upon sporting rights), and maintaining the fences, drains, roads, paths, and gates.

'In fixing the rents, His Grace would seek the advice of a land valuer to be named by the Chairman of the Bedford County Council.[1]

'The Chairman of
   'The ——— Parish Council.'

PARISH 1.—'It was resolved that for the present the Council are not prepared to enter upon the tenancy of ———.'

PARISH 2.—'The subject of allotments was laid before the Council meeting on Monday and carried unanimously that the allotments remain in your hands.'

PARISH 4.—'The Council do not wish to avail themselves of the powers of the Act 1894 to take over the charge of field allotments.'

PARISH 5.—'The Parish Council feel themselves unable to give a definite answer until they have some idea of what the re-valued rents will be.'

PARISH 6.—'The Parish Council cannot at present see their way to accepting the offer.'

[1] At that time the chairman was the late Mr. Charles Howard of Biddenham.

PARISH 7.—' It was unanimously agreed by the Council that, whilst duly appreciating the offer, they beg respectfully to decline it, the Council failing to see what benefits would accrue through the management of the allotments being undertaken by them.'

PARISH 8.—' That the Parish Council, after careful consideration of the offer made of the control of the field allotments in this parish, has reason to believe that the allotment holders are satisfied with the management of the same, and feels itself unable to entertain the matter on the conditions set out in the letter received on January 29 last.

' The Council the more readily adopt this course because they are confident that they can safely trust the important interests of the allottees in the hand of so generous a friend of the labouring classes.'

PARISH 9.—' I am directed by the Council to ask you to convey to His Grace the thanks of the Council for the offer therein contained to transfer to the Council the allotments upon a yearly tenancy, and to say that upon consideration the Council find themselves unable to

accept the offer for the reasons contained in
the Report of the Committee appointed to
consider the matter, which was adopted by the
Council and of which I forward you a copy.'

The following is a copy of the Report of
the Committee of the Parish Council on the
allotment question :

'We find from inquiries made among the
allotment holders and in the town generally
that there is no demand for an increase in the
number of allotments in the parish; rather
the reverse, for a considerable portion of the
allotments in one field are now in the hands of
one person.

'The allotment holders themselves show
no desire to change their present landlord for
the Parish Council.   The only grievances they
appear to have are the highness of rents and
the damage to their crops occasioned by
game.

'With regard to the rents, they allege that
they are too high as compared with the
present rental of allotments in the neighbourhood and land generally, and in the face
of the adverse competition met with from

farmers and nurserymen in realising in local markets.

'From the figures supplied to us it would appear that, irrespective of the question of rent, an allotment is not at the present time remunerative as a commercial undertaking. On certain crops an occasional profit may be made, but on the usually grown crops, viz. potatoes followed by greens, the market prices will not permit of a profit—in fact, an allotment can only be considered as a convenience for producing for home consumption.

'Under these circumstances, and taking into consideration the fact that if the Council were to take over the allotments they would be obliged by the Allotment Acts to let them at such a price as to insure the Council from loss in respect of them, we see no alternative but to report to the Council that it is not advisable for the Council to accept the offer.'

PARISH 10.—'It was unanimously agreed that as the present system is working so very satisfactorily and the people appear to be quite contented, it would be a great mistake for the Parish Council to take them over.

Therefore, if quite agreeable to His Grace the Duke of Bedford to continue as heretofore, the Council prefer leaving the matter in his hands.'

PARISH 11.—'I am instructed to inform you that at the above Council's meeting held last evening the question of taking over the management of the allotments was duly considered, and a resolution passed declining to do so.'

PARISH 12.—'Knowing the readiness of His Grace to meet the legitimate requirements of the parishioners, the Council is of opinion that, could the desire for larger holdings be met by letting land for such a purpose in some suitable and convenient place, it would be advisable for all allotment holders to become direct tenants of His Grace, rather than of the Parish Council.'

PARISH 13 (URBAN DISTRICT COUNCIL).—'I am directed to inform you that, whilst thanking His Grace for his offer, the Council do not see their way at present to accepting it.'

M

CHAPTER VIII

AN EXPERIMENTAL STATION—1. AGRICULTURAL.
2. HORTICULTURAL.   3. EDUCATIONAL

To those who are interested in the science of agriculture a few brief remarks regarding the Woburn experiments, the Experimental Fruit Farm, and the Farm School may be useful.

The Woburn Experimental Farm is one mile distant from Ridgmont Station on the L. & N. W. Railway. It owes its origin to a paper in the Journal of the Royal Agricultural Society written in 1875 by Sir John Lawes and Sir Henry Gilbert, on the subject of the manurial values of purchased foods. This subject subsequently became very prominent and important owing to the passing of the Agricultural Holdings Act of 1875, which, among other measures, provided that compensation to outgoing tenants for the unexhausted value of purchased food should be subject to arbitration. The Council of the Royal

Agricultural Society, seeing the far-reaching effect of the provision, at once endeavoured to correct opinion by experience. After much deliberation the Council at last decided that a grant for an experimental station could not be justified, and the Duke then came forward and agreed to assume the whole cost of the undertaking.

The experimental work, which commenced in 1876, is directed by a special Committee of the Royal Agricultural Society; its scientific side, originally under Sir John Lawes and the late Dr. Voelcker, and subsequently under Dr. Voelcker alone, has, since 1884, been carried on by the latter's son, Dr. J. A. Voelcker. The area of the farm is 131 acres, and from Michaelmas 1877 to March 31, 1896, the total cost of this farm to the estate has been 16,379*l.*, or about 885*l.* per annum. The farm selected for the purpose was well chosen, as furnishing wholly different conditions from those existing on the well-known Rothamsted station. At Rothamsted the land is heavy; at Woburn light and sandy. Starting with the definite object of ascertaining the values of manure obtained by the consumption of different kinds of purchased foods, the Royal Agricultural Society has now extended the field of investigation. Experiments on the continuous growth of wheat and barley ; on clovers, with a view to observing (1) the duration of the life of the clovers in ordinary cultivation, (2) the value of different manures, (3) the relation of manures to clover sickness, were inaugurated, and (4) comprehensive experiments relating to the laying down of permanent pastures were set on foot. Moreover, various trials of fertilisers have been carried out; in 1896 the new specific 'nitragin' was introduced, and yearly experiments have been conducted in the feeding of bullocks and sheep. Twenty years is a short time in the history of an undertaking of this kind, but it is to be hoped that the mass of information thus gathered at Woburn will, ere long, be available to the agricultural interest in the shape of well-digested and practical leaflets.[1]

The Experimental Fruit Farm at Woburn

[1] A detailed account of this Experimental Farm will be found in the Appendix.

was started in 1895 in conjunction with
Spencer Pickering, F.R.S., in whose hands
the whole organisation, both practical and
scientific, has been left. The object of this
institution is not that of supplying a model of
what a fruit farm should be, nor is it that of
testing or demonstrating the possibility of
growing fruit in the district as a commercial
success; its main object is to supply a want
which has been felt by all who have given
serious attention to the culture of fruit, by
providing an establishment where any matters
connected with fruit growing, whether of practical or of purely scientific interest, may be
investigated in a rigorously scientific manner;
it is, in short, an experimental station, where
horticultural questions and problems are dealt
with in the same manner as agricultural questions are at the station of the Royal Agricultural Society.

No such station existed in England, if we
except the Chiswick gardens of the Royal
Horticultural Society, and from this quarter,
chiefly owing to a want of funds, little work
has emanated. Horticultural stations exist

on the Continent and in our colonies, and of the 52 agricultural stations established in the United States many contain horticultural departments; but the greater part of the work done in foreign countries is of little use to English fruit growers, inasmuch as the climate, the varieties of fruit, and many of the insects and fungoid pests are different.

There is, no doubt, something to be said on both sides of the question of whether an institution of this character should be established by the State or by a private individual; but in the absence of State intervention, individual enterprise may yield very profitable results, especially where there is a reasonable prospect, as I trust there may be in this case, of the work being carried on long enough to yield definite results.

Although the endeavour to derive pecuniary profit from the undertaking has never been taken into account, yet the commercial aspects of fruit growing receive consideration at the farm. Certain plots of ground have been planted in ways suitable for farmers, market growers, and cottagers respectively, and careful accounts are kept of each plot separately, so that the cost and profit of the various methods of cropping the ground may be ascertained.

Every investigation, however abstruse or scientific in its nature, must be considered as having a prospective practical value if it tends to increase our general knowledge of the subject, and in this light may be regarded a large number of the questions now under investigation at the farm. There are, for instance, sixty experiments on apple trees, in which different methods of planting, pruning, manuring, &c., are being tested, and the following may be mentioned as an instance of one of the most striking results already obtained. It is a common practice in farmers' orchards all over the country to allow grass to grow round the young trees, but it has been proved by our experiments that this practice reduces the amount of growth of the trees to one-eighth of that of similar trees round which the soil has been kept open.

Apple trees are naturally those which occupy the greater part of the farm, the apple being the most important fruit for English

growers ; but the other fruits which are hardy
and thrive out of doors in England are also
being investigated, and all our experience
hitherto goes to prove that the failure of any
one embarking on fruit growing in the neighbourhood would not be due to any deficiency
of crop. This is important, inasmuch as the
ground on which the farm is situated possesses
but few apparent advantages for fruit growing.
It has a gentle slope to the south-west, but
is much exposed to wind ; the soil is rich, but
it is heavy and shallow, there being only about
nine inches of good soil, below which there is
a bed of very stiff clay ; the ground is mostly
low, with a brook running along the bottom of
it, and the land is retentive of moisture, and
in wet weather becomes quite unworkable ;
indeed, as an arable field, in which condition it
had been for many years previously, it had
acquired an evil reputation, and before its conversion into a fruit farm, had been allowed to
become very foul.

In addition to its experimental side, the
farm is utilised as a nursery where trees are
being raised to furnish a supply to those

tenants on the estate who wish to embark on fruit growing, or to fill up vacancies in existing orchards. There has not, at present, been time enough to develop fully the functions of the fruit farm in relation to the estate, but it is proposed that details of all the orchards on the various estates, whether in Bedfordshire or elsewhere, should be recorded at the fruit farm, so that any application for fruit trees on behalf of the tenants may be dealt with by an experienced person, already possessed of full knowledge of the requirements of the case, and the trees will be supplied direct from the fruit farm, and in many cases planted by, or under the supervision of, the manager. In cases where a tenant, whether farmer or cottager, is embarking in fruit growing for the first time, it is much to his interest, as well as to the interest of the estate, that the work of planting and of tending the trees for the first year should be carried out by experienced persons, and so far as our present experience goes we have found the tenants very ready to avail themselves of these advantages.

Use will probably be made of the fruit

farm for educational purposes in connection
with the County Council farm school, and it
is also proposed, eventually, to give evening or
other lectures on fruit growing for the benefit
of all who may care to attend. It has been
considered advisable, however, not to start any
lectures of this sort till we shall have obtained
from personal experience a better knowledge
of the commercial prospects of fruit growing
in the district, lest we should induce some to
embark on an industry which could not be
conducted successfully. For the same reason
we have been careful to avoid even an appearance of advocating fruit growing for the
farmers, and consider that the initiative should
be left entirely to them.

At present the fruit farm extends over
twenty acres, and nearly the whole of the
ground is already planted. The planting, however, has not been carried out to any great
extent in that close manner which would be
necessary for commercial purposes, for many
of the experiments will not be complete till the
trees have attained maturity, and till they
occupy much more space than they do now,

and any cropping of this space would modify the soil in a manner which might render the results of the experiment doubtful. For this reason alone, independent of expense of the weighings and measurements and other scientific work necessary in experiments, the farm as a whole could never be expected to yield a money profit, or even to pay its expenses; indeed, it is probable that it will cost annually about 500*l*., without charging interest on the capital expenditure. This latter has been about 3,300*l*.

The staff includes a resident manager, and on the average seven or eight men and boys, the amount of labour required varying considerably with the time of year.

Besides the manager's house and the necessary sheds, there is a garden house in the ground which is used for exhibition, lecture, or reception purposes. A store room for the fruit and a new office are in course of erection.

All who are interested in fruit cultivation are gladly welcomed at the farm, which is close to the Ridgmont Station on the London and North-Western Railway.

Among the County Councils which have set themselves to make novel use of the money obtained under the Local Taxation (Customs Excise) Act 1890 (53 and 54 Vict. ch. 60), that of Bedfordshire stands out pre-eminent. Dealing with a county largely devoted to agriculture, the Council has not been content merely to encourage classes in subjects allied to and bearing upon agriculture, but has established a farm school upon the Warren Farm, Ridgmont, on the Woburn Estate.

This enterprise, which was originated by Mr. Theodore Harris,[2] was heartily supported by me. The buildings, specially erected for the accommodation of twenty scholars, at a cost of 3,026*l*., and the land at a nominal rental, were placed at the disposal of the Council. The school is planned on the model farm schools in Zürich and Würtemberg, full and detailed reports on which were obtained on the spot by the organising secretary of the Technical Instruction Committee. The farm school provides instruction in the principles upon which the best farm practice is founded, and combines with

[2] Chairman of the Beds County Council Technical Instruction Committee.

theory daily practical work on the farm, including the care of stock, dairy work and poultry, reaping, bee-keeping, land measuring, ploughing, hedging and ditching, stacking and thatching, and the care and use of machinery. Ten scholarships in each year are offered to the sons of Bedfordshire labourers. The scholarships consist of board, lodging, and instruction at the farm school for two years, and the payment of 'reward wages' of 2s. per week during the first year, and 2s. 6d. a week during the second year. The candidates must be between fifteen and seventeen years of age, Bedfordshire lads of good character, engaged on the land, and give a reasonable assurance that they will afterwards follow farming pursuits. Further requirements are that the lads must be able to read and write fairly well, and they are also expected to show an elementary knowledge of the principles of farm science as taught in an evening agricultural class, under the regulations of the County Council, or so far as is given in Dr. Tanner's 'Primer of Agriculture.'

The universal desire to own a bit of land, which is so marked a feature in continental

countries, enables the educational authorities
in Switzerland to charge a fee of 200 francs
per annum to the farm pupils of Strickhof, the
school near Zürich, which has twice been
inspected by Mr. Spooner[3] on behalf of the
County Council.   The whole cost of the boys'
training   is   defrayed   in   Bedfordshire from
county funds.   A visit to the Ridgmont Farm
shows the plan in full working order.

Turning now to the actual work at the
school, we find that on alternate days the boys
work on the fields or in the homestead, while
in the interval they address themselves to the
theoretical side of their career.   The rules
are simple.   Rising at 5.30 A.M. in summer,
they are thoroughly busy from morning until
night.   The net cost of rations is rather less
than 6s. per head per week, including the staff,
and this low cost is attained after dealing with
the local tradesmen, the authorities not thinking it worth while to deal with the Stores in
London while ratepayers were ready to furnish
adequate supplies on the spot at but a slightly

---

[3] The Secretary of the Beds County Council Technical Instruction Committee.

enhanced cost.   The physical appearance and mental force of the pupils are noteworthy.

The estimate of the sum required for the farm school for the current year is made out as follows :

Household	£327	0	0
Domestic service	35	0	0
Laundry	28	0	0
Coal and oil	30	0	0
Salaries	170	0	0
Rates and taxes	40	0	0
Doctor	10	0	0
Reward wages	78	0	0
	£718	0	0

In addition to this current annual expense the Council has set apart a capital sum of 2,500*l.* for the purposes of working the farm.

The lads take their turn at Sunday work, and by doing so, they are only employed two Sundays out of ten, one for cattle and the other for sheep.

The lad who attends to cattle feeds the pigs and poultry, and when he and the one who attends to sheep have had their breakfast, they join the other lads at farm work until it is time for them to attend to stock at night.

As occasion arises each lad takes his turn

at ploughing, harrowing, hoeing, rolling, sowing, reaping, mowing, stacking, thatching, hedging, ditching, sheep-shearing, and all kinds of farm work as it comes in season.

TABLE FOR FARM WORK

Names	Saturday	Monday	Tuesday	Wednesday	Thursday	Friday
Section A						
A B C D E	Cattle Sheep	Under instruction indoors	Cattle Sheep	Under instruction indoors	Sheep Cattle	Under instruction indoors
Section B						
F G H I J	Under instruction indoors	Cattle Sheep	Under instruction indoors	Cattle Sheep	Under instruction indoors	Sheep Cattle
Section A						
A B C D E	Cattle Sheep	Under instruction indoors	Cattle Sheep	Under instruction indoors	Cattle Sheep	Under instruction indoors
Section B						
F G H I J	Under instruction indoors	Cattle Sheep	Under instruction indoors	Cattle Sheep	Under instruction indoors	Cattle Sheep

TIME TABLE

Bell rings at . . . . 5.30 A.M.
Each lad to be out in the yard 5.50
Breakfast for those turning out with horses, 5.50
    so as to turn out with men at 6.15
Ordinary breakfast 8
Resume work 8.30
Dinner . . . . · 1   P.M.
Resume work 2
In at 6
Tea 6
Supper 8.30
Lights out 9.45

ACREAGE AND CROPPING

The total acreage of the farm is 275 acres, of which 149 are arable and 126 pasture; speaking generally, it is intended to adopt the four course system of cropping, but as the land has been somewhat cross cropped, it will take time before the land is properly apportioned.

At present the cropping stands as follows :—

	Acres	
Wheat	28	good crop
Oats	42	light crop
Barley	26	medium crop
Roots	24	regular but small
Market gardening .	5	good crop
Bare fallow . . .	15	
Beans	7	medium crop
Old clover root . .	7	

N

TIME TABLE OF STUDIES—RIDGMONT FARM SCHOOL

MORNING

	9.15–10	10–10.45	10.45–11.30	11.30–12.30
Monday .	English	General Agricultural Science	Arithmetic	Farm Animals
Tuesday .	" Arithmetic	" Freehand Drawing	" Chemistry	" English
Wednesday				
Thursday .	" Farm Animals	" General Agricultural Science	" "	" Arithmetic
Friday .				
Saturday .	"	"	"	"

AFTERNOON

	2–2.45	2.45–3.30	3.30–4.15	4.15–5
Monday .	Chemistry	Arithmetic	Botany	General Agricultural Science
Tuesday .	" General Agricultural Science	" Botany	" Model Drawing	" Physical Geography
Wednesday				
Thursday .	" English	" "	" Drawing (Geometry)	" Chemistry
Friday .				
Saturday .	"	"	"	"

The staff consists of a house master, his wife, and a bailiff. The house master is responsible for the conduct of the boys at all times during their residence at the school, except when they are working under the eye of the bailiff. The house master's wife acts as matron of the establishment. All indoor studies are carried on under the house master. The bailiff superintends the lads when at farm work. There are three labourers employed, all other labour being found by the lads. There is also a dairy instructress on the staff.

CHAPTER IX

FARMS IN HAND AND THE LAYING DOWN
OF LAND TO GRASS

In reviewing the melancholy history of the last
eighteen years of agriculture in the Midlands,
no feature is more remarkable than the complete failure of the agricultural experts to recog-
nise, at the beginning of the period, the permanent character of the various forces then at
work. None of them enjoyed a higher reputation than the late Mr. W. J. Beadel, M.P. He
was a man to whom all classes interested in
the land looked up with a respect won by
integrity of purpose no less than by singular
proficiency in his profession. But Mr. Beadel,
as will be seen from his report on Farm E, in
the following list of farms in hand, did not
dream that it was possible for the unsatisfactory state of agricultural affairs to continue.

Nor was Mr. Beadel singular in his failure to appreciate the permanent nature of the depression. Agriculturists and the nation at large were alike insensible to the real character of the depression. Nevertheless the causes at work were not obscure even in 1880. The gust of prosperity consequent on the continental wars of 1870 and 1877–78 had spent itself. Cheap marine transport had already thrown open the English market to the cereals of four continents. Machinery was no longer an English monopoly. The depreciation of silver had given to the wheat growers of the East a bounty upon their production. And these elements of the problem, though not exhausting the situation, were sufficient to determine the fate of British agriculture. It is easy to be wise after the event, but it is strange that a catastrophe which was no longer merely impending but had actually taken place should have been regarded by those best able to judge as a passing cloud.

Owing to the frequent recurrence of bad seasons, coupled with low prices and diminishing capital, it was difficult, not to say impossible, for

the tenants of farms consisting of heavy clays
and blowing sands to make headway ; thus arose
urgent appeals for revised rents.   Mr. Beadel
and his school held that it was unwise to lower
rents permanently, as seasons and circumstances might improve—seasons certainly.   In
other respects also he was hopeful, whereas
to make large reductions of rent in this case
and that case without regard to the estate as
a whole must force on a general revaluation ;
for though the circumstances of individual
cases varied materially, yet seasons and prices
were dominant influences, common to all, and
it was not a whit too much to say that the
tenants as a body were fast losing confidence,
and were sustaining great losses, by reason
solely of these influences.

Now a general revaluation at a period of
great depression (possibly, it was hoped, a
passing cloud) was held to be a very grave
step ; for if the conditions improved, it would
not be possible to advance rents of *sitting*
tenants—that is to say, it would *practically*
not be possible—nor could a general revaluation be confined to Beds and Bucks : hence Mr.

Beadel's advice of a policy of remission, assistance in draining, laying down to grass, erection of implement sheds (for which applications
were numerous)—indeed any reasonable concession in order to keep tenants on their legs,
short of permanent reductions.   But where
such assistance would be absolutely useless,
then rather than retain tenants whose farms
were a disgrace, going from bad to worse, a
discouragement and bad example to all, en-
tailing an ultimate accumulation of neglect
that would destroy all confidence and tend to
panic, Mr. Beadel preferred the bold course of
taking such a farm in hand with the object
of restoring its condition, maintaining as
far as possible the rent, and seeking a new
tenant.

The accounts show how great a cost this
step involved; but it should be remembered
that the adverse times pursued the management as they did the outgoing tenants, bad
seasons and low prices still prevailed, nor is it
possible to manage a farm taken in hand
temporarily (in order to bring it into condition)
upon the same scale of expenditure as that of

a sitting tenant. The farm has to be equipped as a going concern on the spur of the moment, and the equipments have to be dispersed by public auction on a re-letting for what they will fetch. For instance, implements which cost 1,730*l.* sold (practically a forced sale) for 725*l.* Outgoing tenants received for acts of husbandry 273*l.* in respect of their *bankrupt* holdings, whereas the landlord received only 209*l.* on re-letting farms *in condition.*[1]

On the Beds and Bucks properties one of the effects of the agricultural depression was to reduce the margin of license permitted in the old times to farmers deficient in skill, energy, or capital.

An analysis of the circumstances on which farms on the Beds Estate in this period reverted to the landowner and involved him in a gross expenditure of 99,264*l.* 4*s.* 3*d.* will perhaps be instructive. The following is a tabular statement of the gross receipts and expenditure.

[1] These amounts were settled by valuers whose decisions could be enforced at law.

BEDS FARMS IN HAND, 1879–1896

Farms	Acreage	Gross Receipts			Gross Expenditure			Deficit			Surplus		
	acres	£	s.	d.	£	s.	d.	£	s.	d.	£	s.	d.
A	275	9,870	16	6	13,100	14	1	3,229	17	7	—		
B	490	15,225	14	11	18,709	6	8	3,483	11	9	—		
C	339	21,543	2	5	28,124	18	9	6,581	16	4	—		
D	200	2,010	10	4	2,528	12	0	518	1	8	—		
E	475	15,271	14	9	20,270	9	9	4,998	15	0	—		
F	212	6,562	14	5	9,075	5	5	2,512	11	0	—		
G	211	3,260	10	2	2,978	19	10	—			281	10	4
H	277	1,099	9	5	1,411	9	2	311	19	9	—		
I	320	1,303	5	0	3,064	8	7	1,761	3	7	—		
Total .		76,147	17	11	99,264	4	3	23,397	16	8	281	10	4

Total net deficit . £23,116 6 4

I also append a statement giving details of area, and the result as expressed in rent of the outlay. The extracts from Mr. Beadel's report which follow should be read in connection with this statement.

EXTRACTS FROM MR. W. J. BEADEL'S REPORT (1879)

FARM A

. . . The way in which the farm has been mismanaged is deplorable to a degree, and disgraceful to the occupier. Portions no doubt require under-draining,

BEDS AND BUCKS ESTATES

Farms in hand from Michaelmas 1870 to Michaelmas 1892

Name of Farm	Acreage when taken in hand			Rent when taken in hand		Date when taken in hand	Date when re-let	Acreage when re-let			Rent when re-let		Rent per acre as revalued in 1893
	Arable	Pasture	Total	Amount	Per acre			Arable	Pasture	Total	Amount	Per acre	
	Acres	Acres	Acres	£ s. d.	s. d.	Mchs.	Mchs.	Acres	Acres	Acres	£ s. d.	s. d.	s. d.
A	236	109	345	480 0 0	27 0	1870	1882	225	120	345	396 0 0	23 0	16 0
B	427	61	489	673 10 0	27 6	1879	1882	364	126	490	505 0 0	20 7	12 3
C	235	87	322	425 10 8	26 4	1881	1889	164	159	323	300 0 0	18 6	—
D	109	95	205	281 0 0	27 6	1881	1882	109	95	205	234 2 0	22 10	15 0
E	230	244	475	645 0 0	27 2	1881	1885	192	216	² 408	408 0 0	20 0	12 6
F	35	158	193	299 19 0	31 0	1886	1892	—	206	³ 206	286 0 0	27 8	—
G	179	32	211	220 0 0	21 0	1884	1887	132	78	211	120 0 0	11 4	10 0

¹ Farm reduced by sixty-six acres. ² Thirteen acres added from adjoining holding.

and where land has been drained thirty or forty years, examination is necessary, to see where the drains are not acting efficiently, and probably intercepting drains may be required. The last two seasons in particular have been unfavourable to the proper cleaning and cultivation of clay land; still nothing, in my opinion, can justify the neglect which seems to have characterised the tenant's mode of farming, or rather mismanagement. The land in course of fallow for this year is one mass of couch, and the farm generally is as full of docks and noxious weeds as can well be imagined.

In other than depressed times of agriculture, such as have been paramount for the last two or three years, the tenant's rent is not in my judgment at all an unfair one.

Under present circumstances two courses are open, viz. :

1. To take the farm in hand, put right the drainage, thoroughly clean the land and get it into condition. This course, excepting from absolute necessity, I certainly should not recommend.

2. To let the farm to a man of capital, who is known to be a good manager, at a progressive rent. For cleaning and getting into proper order the lower portion of the farm time will be required, in addition to which a larger quantity of land will have to be fallowed than ought to be the case, and consequently a loss of profit to the incoming tenant.

I presume that, inasmuch as the tenant is leaving

by arrangement at Michaelmas next, no claim can
be made against him for breaches of covenant and
the foul state in which the land will be left; and even
assuming that a claim can be made, there is no
amount of money which is likely to be awarded,
under the ordinary covenants of a lease or agreement,
which will anything like compensate a landlord for
the pecuniary injury he sustains.

In dealing with a new tenant, much will depend
upon negotiations and the concessions asked by him.
It would not be unwise, I think, to allow half the
first year's rent, providing the new tenant fallowed,
in a thoroughly clean and husbandmanlike manner,
at least one-fourth part of the heavy portion of the
arable land during the first year of his tenancy.
This would at all events secure that portion being
in a fit state to go through a course of cropping, with
ordinary skill and care. For the second and third
years, concessions in rent should also be made, but
to a more modified degree; after which, unless agriculture in the United Kingdom is to continue under
a cloud as at present, and the occupation of land
cease to be reasonably remunerative, I see no reason
why the present rent should not be reverted to.
Putting right the drainage must, I fear, fall upon
the landlord, without a reasonable prospect of obtaining interest on the outlay.

FARM B (1879)

. . . The entire farm is in a very foul state, many of the fields being full of docks and other noxious weeds. Portions of the strong land appear to have been drained, but from some cause or other the drainage is either worn out or working imperfectly. The foundation of all improvement necessitates this being put right, as also under-draining such other portions of the land as require it. . . .

. . . I was informed that scab has been prevalent in the flock of sheep on this farm. If true, this is a serious matter, and would prevent any prudent man from having sheep upon the farm until the land has had time to become purified by exposure to weather and constant cultivation.

The principal objection to this farm is that there is an insufficiency of pasture. Such as there is lies near the house, and so far is convenient for occupation. Should the farm be taken in hand, as I understand has been determined, it would be desirable to lay down more land to grass, and I would suggest more particularly fields Nos. 201, 203, and 311 being so treated.

The situation of the farm, character of house, and convenience of the homestead ought to command a first-class tenant at all ordinary times; but we are living now in exceptionally depressed times, when there are more farms to let than applicants for them.

Under these circumstances, I do not consider this farm in its present condition will let at what, otherwise, may be considered its fair ordinary value ; and should the farm not be in hand, concession in rent will have to be made for two or three years.

In my judgment 600*l.* a year, tithe free, represents the fair value of the farm, the landlord undertaking at his own expense (and without charging interest) to carry out such drainage as he may consider necessary.

FARM C (1880)

. . . Much of the arable is in a very foul state. Mr. Z. grows white clover and alsike for seeds. Two fields more particularly, Nos. 152 and 167, are in a disgraceful state, full of docks which are just ready to drop their seed. The fallows are not all well made, and there is a want of management and tidiness pervading the farm which is anything but creditable to an occupier. . . .

. . . Under ordinary circumstances, I should not hesitate advising a landlord to give a tenant such as Mr. Z. notice to quit, unless he altered his mode of farming and managed his land in a clean and proper manner. . . .

. . . Including interest upon draining, I am of opinion that the fair annual value of this occupation is three hundred and sixty-five pounds (365*l.*) ; but I should not recommend any reduction being made in rent to Mr. Z. whilst he farms as he does.

FARM D (1880)

. . . I have rarely been over an occupation where there has been such an utter absence of ordinary care, and where gross mismanagement, possibly from want of knowledge or repeated disappointment, is so apparent. . . .

. . . The present rent cannot be expected to be realised, at all events unless times alter very much indeed for the better, and then only after the land has been got into a proper state of cultivation.

This is really a case where circumstances as they arise must determine the letting value, and where not being able to do what one would like, to do the best one can.   The farm can of course be taken in hand and the land put into order, but allowance of rent to a fresh tenant will be by far the least expensive course.

FARM E (1881)

. . . Before entering into further detail I would observe that this is a most unsatisfactory occupation. The soil, with slight exception, is strong, tenacious clay.   The north-eastern, eastern, and southern portions broken ground, much of it very heavily timbered, the quantity therefore available for profitable occupation must be considerably discounted. The northern portion is very strong land, lies low, and during the past wet seasons has not only been unproductive, but must have involved considerable loss upon the occupier.

I understand Mr. X. has been allowed 100*l.* a year during the time he has occupied the farm (now four years), in order to enable him to get the arable land into proper cultivation, its state at the time of his entry being very foul. This allowance has not produced the desired effect, not from any want of exertion or desire on the part of the tenant to carry out that which he undertook, nor from any want of supervision on the part of an agent, but solely and entirely from recent ungenial seasons, which have prevented land of so tenacious a character from being cleaned, or the labour bestowed thereon yielding that benefit which under even ordinarily fair seasons would have been the case. This remark must not be considered as applicable to No. 114 and part of No. 116 on plan : this land is in a discreditable state. The only excuse to be offered is that every effort was made to get the stronger and lower land into order first, and had seasons been fairly good the tenant probably would have been able to remedy this complaint, if not entirely, at all events partially.

Unpleasant as is such a state of things, and much as one regrets it, the above explanation is the true one.

Compact as this farm is, with house and buildings in the centre, fences straight, fields large, and situate so near to ——, it is difficult to imagine its not readily letting, and at a full rent; but with the past wet seasons, and the losses consequent upon a con-. tinued low average price for wheat, I fear there will be very considerable difficulty at present in finding a solvent man to hire unless at a very low rent, and indeed on pretty nearly his own terms. An intending tenant will take into account the fact, and fairly so, that although the total quantity is 401 a. 2 r. 17 p., ten per cent. at the least, or in round figures 40 acres, must be deducted for roads, waste, timber, &c., leaving 360 acres, or about that quantity, as the area from which he will have to provide rent, interest of capital, and tenant's profit.

A tenant in these times will be very shy of hiring such a farm if he can procure one where, with the same capital employed, the expense of cultivation would be less and the risk of disappointment as well as the anxiety not so great.

As to re-letting, considering the weather of the past month (more rain having fallen during that period than has previously been recorded for years), I should advise no steps being taken towards finding a successor to Mr. X., beyond mentioning the fact that the farm will be vacant at Michaelmas next.

Should the autumn be favourable, and prices improve during the winter, farmers may in the spring be induced to anticipate brighter prospects and entertain hiring heavy land.

It surely must be impossible for the present unsatisfactory state of agricultural affairs to continue. Rent is not the main consideration, and represents

o

but a small portion of either profit or loss. What to suggest for the best is difficult. In order to bring the occupation within the reach of a greater number, I think it would be not unwise to separate Nos. 118, 119, 120, and 121, containing 66 a. 2 r. 19 p., from this farm. There should be no difficulty in finding tenants for this portion (all grass) even under the most unfavourable circumstances ; and, assuming no tenant to come forward willing to hire them, the crop of grass with the after-feed to December 25 could be sold each year until a demand for land of that description again arises. This farm would, by this plan, be reduced from 401 a. 2 r. 37 p. to 335 a. 0 r. 18 p.

At the present time I do not think a better rent can be expected than five hundred and twenty pounds (520l.) per annum for the farm as now held ; or, if divided,

For the 335 a. 0 r. 18 p.   400l. per annum.
„   „   66 a. 2 r. 19 p.   120l. „   „

An allowance from the 400l. for one or two years, in order to meet the unproductive outlay to which an incoming tenant will be subject, must, I fear, be anticipated.

THE LAYING DOWN OF LAND TO GRASS

The fall in the value of wheat and other grain, and the consequent conversion of arable land into pasture, has gravely affected the social and economic conditions of English rural life. The causes of the fall are not far to seek. The average cost of cultivating an acre of wheat in the Punjab is stated to be 14s. 7d. In Canada, Argentina, and South Russia, where the climate is favourable, and where the obligations imposed by the State on the owners of the soil are of a simple nature, the production of wheat is still a profitable business.

The gradual diminution of the production of wheat in this country is scarcely appreciated by the town population; and the consequences of the extinction of the home-grown wheat supply are unlikely to be driven home to the inhabitants of these islands by anything less than the catastrophe of war and famine prices. In 1874 there were under permanent pasture in Great Britain 13,178,012 acres; in 1894 there were 16,465,069. For every 200 acres of arable land converted into pasture, we may assume that five labourers are displaced. If we compare the first and the last periods we find that 82,175 labourers with their families

have been displaced, earning an annual income
of about 2,843,255*l*.

While on the one hand the process of
conversion is prejudicial to the welfare of the
agricultural labourers, on the other hand it is
by no means clear that the substitution of
pasture for cereal cultivation is profitable to
the landowners.   So far as the experience
afforded by the history of these estates is a
guide, the process in question is certainly
unprofitable, and is not apparently accompanied by any corresponding advantages to
the labourers or the landlord.   As recent Blue-
books show, the profits of the grazier are
principally absorbed by the middleman and the
railways.   Two examples may be given of the
financial results to the owner of creating permanent pasture.   One of these cases occurred
on the Beds and Bucks Estates, the other was
at Wansford in Northamptonshire.

In 1881 the ninth Duke, anxious to gain
experience in this direction, laid down some
land to grass near Woburn, under the advice
of one of the greatest authorities on the subject.   The opinion given by him was that if

you only did the work well, and spared no
expense to start with, the good grasses would
maintain themselves, and the process would
be successful. The land cost 10*l*. 0*s*. 6*d*. an
acre to lay down, and a further 5*l*. per acre for
incidental and necessary outlay, and in the
valuation in 1895 it stood at 5*s*. an acre.

The land was in hand at the time, and in
order to avoid any mistake two eminent experts were consulted as to the best methods of.
conditioning the land, and the prescription of
the seeds to be employed. In addition to the
10*l*. 0*s*. 6*d*. per acre actually expended on the
preparation of the soil and the sowing of grass
seed, a considerable outlay was incurred for
the additional fencing rendered indispensable
by the conversion of arable to pasture land.
Further expense was caused by the necessity
for 'renovating mixtures' .of seeds, sown in
order to supply the place of perished grasses.
Draining and manuring operations were also
undertaken, and there were expenses of supervision. Those additional expenses, although
not strictly a part of the prime cost of laying
down the land to grass, were necessary to the

operation. The total cost came therefore to the sum named, and the rental of 5s. per acre was a disastrous result of the operation.

STATEMENT SHOWING COST OF LAYING 64½ ACRES OF ARABLE LAND TO PERMANENT PASTURE IN 1881–82

	The Lawn, 38½ Acres					New Ground, 26 Acres					
	£	s.	d.	£	s.	d.	£	s.	d.	£	s.	d.
Ordinary ploughings and cultivations . .	58	17	9				57	15	0			
Steam ploughings and cultivations . .	74	15	6				45	18	0			
Extra ploughing, cultivations, and couchings	68	15	10				33	14	4			
				202	9	1				137	7	4
Grass seeds .	56	2	11				37	18	4			
Labour and sowing seeds .	1	2	6					15	2			
				57	5	5				38	13	6
Rent, 2 years to Michaelmas 1882, at 27s.6d. per acre per annum . .	105	17	6				71	10	0			
Taxes, 2 years to Michaelmas 1882, at 10s.5d. per acre . .	20	1	0				13	10	10			
				125	18	6				85	0	10
Total outlay . . .				385	13	0				261	1	8
Cost per acre . . .				10	0	4				10	0	10
Average cost per acre . . £10 0 6												

The primary cost of laying down land to grass is as a rule considerable, for the simple reason that it is usually carried out on strong clay land, not sufficiently remunerative to continue under cultivation, and, more often than not on land in so foul a state as to necessitate a summer's dead fallowing with repeated cultivations.

From estate records I find that between the years 1862 and 1866, 549 acres of forest [4] at Wansford were cleared and grubbed at a cost of 8,139*l.* 18*s.* 4*d.*, there being an additional outlay of 1,207*l.* 12*s.* 11*d.* on fencing, 3,094*l.* 0*s.* 8*d.* on under-draining, 1,226*l.* 3*s.* 3*d.* on roads, 5,229*l.* 17*s.* 9*d.* on buildings and cottages, and several other items, amounting in all to a total expenditure of 21,047*l.* 10*s.* 1*d.* Against this substantial sum, receipts came in amounting to 13,496*l.* 17*s.* 10*d.*, leaving therefore a deficit of 7,529*l.* 12*s.* 5*d.* This woodland was transformed into two farms, one let at 20*s.* and the other at 25*s.* per acre. Being rich with leaf-mould, enormous crops of cereals were produced for the first few years ; but, on

[4] The Bedford Purlieus, part of the old Forest of Rockingham.

the exhaustion of the virgin soil, they resumed the unfruitful condition that no doubt was the occasion of their being afforested in the first instance. These farms were let about five years ago at a rent of 200*l*. per annum, the arable land being in a disgraceful state and, with the exception of 81 acres which were properly laid down, in a very foul condition (there being no other artificially sown grass on the farm). Upwards of 200 acres were allowed to go out of cultivation and seed themselves down. On the tenant giving up the farms they were let to fresh tenants, but were given up by them at Lady Day 1893 on account of the losses incurred in cultivation.

As the major portion of the land was quite unsuitable for cultivation, even in far better times than then existed, it was decided to lay it down to permanent pasture, and the several fields were annually let by auction. The operations commenced by sowing seeds, together with a light crop of mustard on 58 acres of the cleanest parts of the farms, as well as on some land which had already been sown

with wheat; and the remainder of the arable
land, 157 acres in extent, was steam-cultivated
several times and summer-fallowed, the grass
seeds being sown the following year with
mustard and barley crops.

It may be useful to have a comparison of
the letting prices of the *self-sown* portions of
these farms in comparison with those portions
which have been sown with artificial grasses.
Taking these for the years 1894, 1895, and 1896,
the average of the former was only 5s. 8d.
per acre, and of the latter 16s. 3d. per acre,
the one being *three* times as valuable as the
other.

In regard to the interesting phenomenon
of the reassertion of the forest grasses,[5] in the
case of the land that has been allowed to sow
itself after being under cultivation it is not
noticeable in any marked degree, the assertion
being more on the part of those grasses that
are natural to poor soils of a similar character;
however, on a portion of one of the farms that
has never been under cultivation at all the
forest grasses are very marked, although grazing

[5] Cf. Dr. Fream's note at end of chapter.

from year to year has induced trefoil and other grasses indigenous to the soil. During the last few years the herbage on the poor self-sown parts of the farms has improved in the most surprising degree, simply because of the more careful grazing ; the number of horses has been restricted ; and the different fields, being annually let by auction, have very little rough grass left on them, and where the improvement especially lies, they are cleared of all stock for *five months* from December 1 each year.

In districts where land naturally and easily takes to grass, there is no doubt whatever of the advisability of doing the work with the greatest care, in the best possible manner, and without stinting the cost; for in such circumstances the grass, once started, quickly establishes itself, and the better the start the earlier and more satisfactory the return.

The laying down of grass under these conditions is not difficult, and the procedure is well understood by practical men. It is not often, however, that land is laid to grass when the quality is good enough to justify keeping it under the plough.

The problem is, how to produce pasture on the extremes of light and heavy soils when abandoned for corn growing.

On the Beds and Bucks Estates 1,308 acres have been laid to grass since the year 1880 by the landlord, either by finding permanent grass seeds, or by doing the work himself.

Besides this there is a large area which has been sown down by tenants themselves, or which has been allowed to 'tumble down.'

The subject has been given a good deal of attention, and on p. 204 are given particulars of several methods which have been tried, with an account of the outlay incurred.

It will be noticed that the heaviest expenditure has not produced a remarkable increase of value at the present time, and the value of these ' grass ' lands compares very unfavourably with their value in days of corn-growing prosperity.

The laying of these lands to 'grass' therefore does not appear to be satisfactory or encouraging from a capitalist's point of view,

Date	Farm	Acre-age	Cost per Acre	Rental in 1878[a]	Rental per Acre in 1895	Remarks
1881	A	11	*s. d.* 29 0	*s. d.* 27 9	*s. d.* 15 0	Heavy soil. Laid to grass by landlord during time farm was in hand. Seeds only charged to laying down
1883	B {	22 28	54 0 } 30 0 }	28 0	7 6	Very heavy clay land ; grew good wheat and beans. Rental in 1880, 28*s.* per acre
1882 1881	C D	12 26	130 0 } 130 0 }	32 8	11 0	Heavy clay. Sown down, under expert advice, without a corn crop after a bare fallow
1884 1886 1878	} E F	12 12	30 0 } 29 0 }	32 6	{ 13 0 { 15 0	Seeds only provided by landlord. Tenant did work ; all sown with a crop under the advice of experts as to seeds
1881 1880	G H	12 20	129 0 } 29 8 }	27 6	{ 12 0 { 12 0	Sown down without a corn crop, under expert advice as to seeds. Part with and part without a corn crop. Former most expensive
1888 1889	I J	35½ 7½	112 3 } 34 2 }	15 0	{ 12 to { 15	Laid down when farm in hand. Heavy cost was for cleaning
1881 1882	K	64½	200 6	27 6	5 0	Details already supplied, p. 198

[a] The values of 1878 are the average rent of the farms, as no field-to-field valuation was made at that time, but the values quoted would not be very far out probably.

and the operation is less desirable when the effect of the process upon labour in a district is taken into account.

It appears to be impossible to convert these soils into really satisfactory pastures. They lack the ' humus ' necessary for the food of the best grasses ; and unless this is artificially provided by heavy manuring, top dressings, and, in the case of sands, claying or marling, they are failures as grass.

They can be treated as above, and no doubt it is possible to point to a lawn or small paddock near home which is satisfactory. But at what cost ? A lawn is one thing ; thousands of acres another, and the cost must be taken into account in a large undertaking, when it will be found prohibitive. The matter was investigated at Woburn in the early part of this century by George Sinclair,[7] who describes ' transplanting ' grasses (the system we now know as ' inoculation'). This is a success ; but the secret is, that the depth of soil or ' humus ' is increased thereby. The cost, how-

---

[7] George Sinclair, F.L.S., F.H.S., *Hortus Gramineus Woburnensis*, 1825.

ever, places the system out of the question. I
have come to the conclusion that it is unwise
to go to great expenditure on these lands—
either as to expensive seeds or elaborate cultivation and cleaning—as an outlay of 30s. an
acre will probably produce as good a result as
if 10l. were spent. It is best to accept the
situation, and admit that these lands must
revert to the condition they were in before
the then high price of corn justified their being
broken up and brought into cultivation. If
they only produce a rental of 5s. an acre it is
more profitable for the landowner and farmer
than if the latter lost 5l. an acre by corn
growing. Whether the interests of labour are
served, however, is another question. But,
since the present value of cereals is the main
factor in the problem, it is foreign to my
purpose here to discuss that aspect of the
question.

The following note, written by Dr. W.
Fream, on the herbage of the Wood Farms,
dated February 26, 1897, is appended.

The problem to be dealt with may be stated as follows :

Land on certain farms was laid down to grass with a known seed mixture some years ago, and land on other similar farms was allowed to lay itself down. It is desired to know how far the artificially sown grasses have been ousted by others indigenous to the district, and whether the artificially sown pastures are more valuable now than the others.

I proceed to notice very briefly the characteristic features of the herbage—so far as distinguishable at this early period of the season—in some of the fields I inspected.

No. 9. Old field, about 85 acres.—The portion of this field bordering the road was occupied by exceedingly poor herbage, prominent amongst the grasses being the fine bent grass, or twitch, *Agrostis vulgaris*, and the woolly soft grass, or Yorkshire fog, *Holcus lanatus*. Moss was plentiful, and there was an abundance of hawkweed (species of *Hieracium*) and of the wiry rock rose (species of *Helianthemum*), both of which are indicative of poverty of soil. The inner parts of the field where basic slag had been applied had obviously benefited from the dressing; the gramineous herbage was greener and fresher, and it had been more closely grazed. In addition, there was a marked development of trefoil, *Medicago lupulina*, a leguminous plant, known also by such names as black medick and 'hop,' the seed of which

is sometimes sown with that of rye grass to provide
early summer folding for sheep.   Examination of
the roots of the trefoil revealed the presence of the
nodules associated with the abstraction of nitrogen
from the air.   Hence, as a result of dressing with
basic slag, it may be concluded that the condition of
the soil is undergoing improvement, and that the
gradual accumulation of nitrogen by the leguminous
species will lead ultimately to the production of
better and more valuable herbage.

No. 6A. 18 acres.   Sown to grass with a mustard
crop in 1893, and has been once mown.—The most
striking features in the gramineous herbage were
the abundance of cocksfoot grass, *Dactylis glomerata*,
and the fair proportion of ryegrass, *Lolium perenne*.
Red clover, *Trifolium pratense*, and alsike, *Trifolium
hybridum*, were also in evidence, but there was not
much indication of the presence of white or Dutch
clover, *Trifolium repens*.   The seeds sown four years
ago appear, therefore, to be holding their own against
what may be called the indigenous herbage as seen
in the unimproved part of field No. 9.

No. 10. About 34 acres. Laid away to grass
some seventeen years ago, but the work badly done.
—The creeping stems of white clover were seen
here, as also the freely tillering perennial ryegrass,
but there was a considerable quantity of bent grass,
Agrostis.   Whether this latter undesirable constituent was due to the imperfect manner in which the
field was originally laid away to grass, or whether it

is the result of a subsequent invasion, it is impossible to say.

No. 2A. About 25 acres. Laid down eleven years ago, the seed being furnished to the tenant on condition that he got the land clean.—Calls for no special remark, save that the herbage contained an abundance of mouse-ear chickweed, *Cerastium triviale*; but as this is a fairly common constituent in meadows and pastures, no importance need be attached to its presence.

Nos. 1 and 1A. 113 acres. Self-seeded after corn, thirty years ago.—The herbage was here again very 'benty,' though *Agrostis* was apparently not so abundant as in No. 9. A feature in the gramineous herbage was the large amount of dogstail grass, *Cynosurus cristatus*, which occurred here to an extent not noticed in any other field. The poor condition of the soil was shown in a plentiful display of coltsfoot, *Tussilago Farfara*, and of cinquefoil (species of *Potentilla*). The useful effects following the application of basic slag were well seen in this field.

No. 2. 40 acres. Laid down with a mustard crop in 1893.—By far the most prominent feature here was the abundance of cocksfoot grass, which certainly seems to have maintained its position against all rivals. The surface was mossy in places.

No. 11A. About 38 acres. Laid down with a mustard crop in 1894; mown in 1895; grazed in 1896.—The most conspicuous feature in the herbage was again cocksfoot, but it was usefully associated

P

with considerable quantities of the red and white clovers.

If a comparison be instituted between such fields as 9 and 1 and 1A, containing what may be regarded as the indigenous herbage, and such recently seeded fields as 6A, 2, and 11A, the question as to how far the artificially sown grasses have been ousted by the less valuable indigenous species must be answered very decidedly in favour of the artificially sown pastures. Plants included in the mixture with which the latter were seeded down are strongly in evidence upon them, but are rarely noticeable in the old original fields. On the other hand, the comparatively worthless grasses and miscellaneous herbage of the old fields do not appear to have made any successful invasion of the newly laid down pastures.

As to the comparative value of the two groups of pastures, the newly seeded fields have altogether a better 'face,' and an inspection like that which I had the opportunity of making could not lead to any other conclusion than that the new pastures are much superior.

It is not desired to convey the impression that the new pastures have reached a condition of stability as regards the botanical constitution of their herbage. Few pastures anywhere, even the oldest and richest, throw up exactly the same relative proportions of species year after year. It has been proved by the Rothamsted experiments, extending over many years, that a given quantity of the gross produce of the mixed herbage of permanent grass land may be one thing in one season and quite another in another season, both as to the proportion of the different species composing it and as to their condition of development and maturity. Nevertheless, with a continuance of the treatment which the newly seeded pastures have been receiving, it may be anticipated that the struggle will be more of the nature of an internecine strife between the useful species that were included in the seed mixtures with which they were laid down than between these desirable plants and the almost worthless species which so largely occupy the old fields. At the same time, these latter species, which may reasonably be regarded as constituting the native flora of the soil, will ever be ready to take advantage of any lowering in condition of the soil, whether induced by management or by seasonal variations.

A separate reference must be made to the effects —in some cases, the striking effects—of dressings of basic slag. Supplying, as it does, phosphorus and lime to these strong soils, it encourages the growth of leguminous plants. These, obtaining their nitrogen freely from the atmosphere, enrich the soil in this indispensable element by the decay of their roots, and so bring the land into a condition better adapted to the profitable growth of gramineous herbage which is dependent for its nitrogen upon the available supplies of this constituent which are present in the soil.

APPENDIX

THE EXPERIMENTAL FARM AT WOBURN

THE primary set of experiments, known as the 'Rotation Experiments,' were commenced in 1876. The immediate practical object was to see whether the high manurial value assigned in Lawes and Gilbert's 'Tables' to a food very rich in nitrogen, like decorticated cotton cake, as against the much lower value assigned to a food comparatively poor in nitrogen, like maize meal, was borne out in actual practice. In other words, the aim was to discover what was the increase in crops produced respectively by the two foods.

To the 'Rotation Experiments' many others have been, from time to time, added. Thus, since 1877 experiments have been conducted on the continuous growing of wheat and also of barley, year after year, with different artificial manures and with farmyard manure. These experiments are practically a repetition, but on the very different soil of Woburn, of the famous experiments of Lawes and Gilbert on the heavy soil of Rothamsted. As a whole, the results have furnished direct confirmation of the conclusions arrived at from the Rothamsted experiments. The growing of different clover crops has also been investigated, chiefly with a view to testing the duration of the life of clovers, the influence of manures, and the question of 'clover sickness.'

The 'permanence' of different kinds of ryegrass, and the utility of certain fodder crops, such as *Lathyrus sylvestris*, lucerne, &c., have also been tried in this field, and, quite recently, experiments have been conducted here and in other fields on the use of the new inoculating material 'Nitragin' for leguminous crops. The growing of lucerne, in particular, has met with much success.

On other fields of the farm numerous experiments have, from time to time, been conducted, among these being experiments on :—(1) Green-manuring for corn crops ; (2) the growing of different varieties of barley and other crops ; (3) the prevention of 'potato disease' ; (4) the cure of 'finger and toe' in turnips. Another series of experiments comprises the laying down of land to permanent pasture and its subsequent treatment, and the improvement of old pasture. The subject of ensilage has been exhaustively investigated, both as regards the comparative yields of grass as green silage and as hay, and in their feeding results on cattle. A set of silos was erected by the ninth Duke in the Park at the Heath Farm, in order that these experiments might be carried out with completeness.

Lastly, almost since the inception of the experiments, there have been carried out, year by year, experiments on the feeding of bullocks and of sheep, with the object of ascertaining the comparative feeding values of different purchased foods, of new feeding materials, of home-grown foods, and of different rations and quantities of foods.   Papers dealing with the results of these experiments are, from time to time, published in the Journal of the Royal Agricultural Society, and already form a considerable series of records.   It is now intended to supplement the field experiments by the establishment, at the farm, of a ' pot-culture ' station, where scientific investigation will be carried out on crops grown in pots, according to the system which has been found so beneficial on the Continent.   A chemical laboratory will also be included in the new buildings about to be erected.

BEDS AND BUCKS ESTATES

STATEMENT OF INCOME AND EXPENDITURE

1816 TO 1895 INCLUSIVE

STATEMENT OF INCOME AND

INCOME

Year	Acreage			Rents received	Woods and Plantations	Income from other Sources	To[tal] Inc[ome]
	Estate	Woods and Plantations	Total				
	Acres	Acres	Acres	£	£	£	£
1816	—		28,292	28,681	8,514	100	37,
1817	—		28,343	33,530	8,432	1,028 [1]	42,
1818	—		28,341	31,766	9,790	962 [1]	42,
1819	—.		28,604	30,337	9,556	· 273	40,
1820	—		28,810	30,357	10,542	189	41,
1821	—		28,809	30,081	8,122	1,212 [1]	39,
1822	—		28,958	32,301	9,112	483	41,
Half year's Rent of a division of the Estate on change of date of entry			—	7,891	—	—	7,
1823	—		28,958	29,761	9,717	231	39,
1824	—		29,066	28,923	12,093	376	41,
1825	—		29,093	28,738	10,305	463 [1]	39,
1826	—		29,095	28,075	8,981	447 [1]	37,
1827	—		29,117	28,053	9,647	1,790 [1]	39,
1828	—		29,220	29,073	6,821	5,148 [1]	41,
1829	—		29,286	28,259	8,974	223	37,
1830	—		29,286	29,552	9,673	2,979 [1]	42,
1831	—		29,516	29,196	9,921	1,043 [1]	40,
1832	—		29,516	29,745	9,372	708 [1]	39,
1833	—		29,993	29,301	9,692	773 [1]	39,
1834	—		30,003	28,635	8,402	856 [1]	37,
1835	—		29,997	28,329	8,059	1,286 [1]	37,
				600,584	185,725	20,570	806

In these earlier years the Acreages of Woods are included in Estate Totals

[1] Includes

EXPENDITURE, 1816 TO 1895 (*inclusive*)

EXPENDITURE (*excluding Store-yard, Brick-kiln, and Establishments*)

Taxation	Repairs and Maintenance	New Works and Permanent Improvements	Other Expenditure (including Management)	Woods and Plantations	General		Total Expenditure	Net Income
					Churches and Schools (including Works)	Pensions, Compassionate Allowances, Charities, and other General Payments		
£	£	£	£		£	£	£	£
5,740	4,646	500	2,305		17	784	13,992	23,303
4,968	6,700	—	2,696¹		17	1,019	15,400	27,590
4,267	4,800	—	2,998¹		17	733	12,815	29,703
4,631	5,939	—	2,589¹		57	660	13,876	26,290
4,173	8,388	—	2,541	In these earlier years Expenditure on Woods was not shown separately, but was included under the Estate Headings	42	775	15,919	25,169
4,803	6,643	1,050	3,423¹		24	723	16,666	22,749
5,224	7,901	536	2,603		29	664	16,957	⎫ 28,933
1,267	1,967	—	618		19	26	3,897	⎭
4,921	6,870	—	1,900		23	692	14,406	25,303
5,050	10,492	637	2,451		26	649	19,305	22,087
4,926	10,745	—	2,092		12	927	18,702	20,804
5,112	7,426	931	1,853		344	672	16,338	21,165
4,439	6,887	5,866	3,610¹		129	1,055	21,986	17,504
5,107	10,219	942	8,989¹		64	911	26,232	14,810
4,648	10,915	5,352	2,067		83	931	23,996	13,460
5,915	20,691	2,652	7,847¹		436	998	38,539	3,665
5,445	15,318	831	4,744¹		546	755	27,639	12,521
5,256	15,469	3,540	3,716¹		99	862	28,942	10,883
5,082	10,179	3,575	3,156¹		135	780	22,907	16,859
4,954	8,064	3,880	3,597¹		80	619	21,194	16,699
4,958	8,612	939	3,059¹		829	539	18,936	18,738
100,886	188,871	31,231	68,854	—	3,028	15,774	408,644	398,235

Farms in hand.

INCOME

Year	Acreage			Rents received	Woods and Plantations	Income from other Sources
	Estate	Woods and Plantations	Total			
	Acres	Acres	Acres	£	£	£
1836			29,996	30,062	8,978	437 [1]
1837	—		30,008	27,102	10,823	274
1838	—		30,017	27,120	8,614	236
1839	—	In these earlier years the Acreages of Woods are included in Estate Totals.	29,967	27,212	10,659	298
1840	—		30,328	29,356	13,237	228
1841	—		30,328	29,556	12,546	495
1842	—		33,994	34,117	9,812	786
1843	—		34,059	35,041	12,506	910
1844	—		32,622	35,408	11,713	653
1845	—		32,347	35,898	12,180	1,129
1846	—		32,335	35,408	26,446	832
1847	—		32,324	35,514	11,982	805
1848	—		32,322	36,384	10,554	999
1849	—		32,477	35,836	11,059	926
1850	—		32,710	36,932	11,267	1,372 [1]
1851	—		32,744	34,816	9,484	1,185 [1]
1852	—		32,784	33,707	8,607	1,793 [1]
1853	—		32,886	33,359	8,499	2,041 [1]
1854	—		33,162	34,749	9,790	948 [1]
1855	—		33,229	37,002	10,409	787
				664,579	229,165	17,134

EXPENDITURE (*excluding Store-yard, Brick-kiln, and Establishments*)

Taxation	Repairs and Maintenance	New Works and Permanent Improvements	Other Expenditure (including Management)	Woods and Plantations	General		Total Expenditure	Net Income
					Churches and Schools (including Works)	Pensions, compassionate Allowances, Charities, and other general Payments		
£	£	£	£	£	£	£	£	£
5,183	10,885	1,950	2,495		209	889	21,611	17,866
5,155	12,072	1,171	1,950		205	642	21,195	17,004
5,091	10,243	858	2,286		736	822	20,036	15,934
5,375	11,079	194	2,442		191	887	20,168	18,001
5,286	5,329	2,765	1,648	See Note on preceding page.	456	653	16,137	26,684
5,576	5,011	4,132	2,138		185	654	17,696	24,901
7,270	6,887	6,638	2,143	4,190	185	659	27,972	16,743
7,494	7,449	12,272	2,080	5,290	220	1,948	36,753	11,704
7,375	9,332	10,414	1,929	4,801	458	1,797	36,106	11,668
7,310	9,509	13,413	2,212	4,530	329	1,635	38,938	10,269
7,276	8,432	12,477	1,971	5,646	392	1,581	37,775	24,911
7,190	5,861	14,909	2,017	4,976	474	1,976	37,403	10,898
7,475	6,380	14,254	1,912	4,629	497	1,677	36,824	11,113
7,376	6,222	11,548	1,911	4,433	547	1,498	33,535	14,286
7,540	6,313	17,249	2,570 [1]	3,925	654	2,209	40,460	9,111
7,460	5,068	15,387	3,346 [1]	4,229	507	1,533	37,530	7,955
7,333	4,461	14,181	2,937 [1]	3,942	740	1,757	35,351	8,756
7,406	6,375	16,049	3,073 [1]	4,153	643	1,825	39,524	4,375
7,754	6,170	11,063	1,835	4,379	618	2,360	34,179	11,308
8,368	5,596	13,728	1,986	4,812	601	1,620	36,711	11,487
136,293	148,674	194,652	44,881	63,935	8,847	28,622	625,904	284,974

'arms in hand.

INCOME

Year	Acreage			Rents received	Woods and Planta- tions	Income from other Sources
	Estate	Woods and Planta- tions	Total			
	Acres	Acres	Acres	£	£	£
1856	—		33,251	38,597	6,868	1,061
1857	—		33,847	41,113	8,052	1,142
1858	—		33,847	42,603	10,753	1,513
1859	—		34,232	41,837	10,693	1,002
1860	—		34,526	40,548	11,075	640
1861	—		34,539	41,822	9,600	675
1862	—		34,523	42,347	9,125	620
1863	—		34,801	43,633	7,861	466
1864	—		34,841	41,595	7,491	423
1865	—		34,891	40,130	7,345	434
1866	—		34,900	40,890	5,830	379
1867	—		34,953	43,149	4,591	681
1868	—		34,980	46,886	4,049	784
1869	—		34,959	47,623	4,314	1,566
1870	—		35,008	43,543	2,864	610
1871	—		35,022	43,293	3,074	810
1872	—		35,126	45,881	4,575	1,406
1873	32,452	4,293	36,745	48,178	5,926	693
1874	32,837	4,292	37,129	49,849	6,873	977
1875	32,850	4,289	37,139	49,205	7,348	515
				872,722	138,307	16,597

In these earlier years the Acreages of Woods are included in Estate Totals

EXPENDITURE (*excluding Store-yard, Brick-kiln, and Establishments*)

ıxation	Repairs and Maintenance	New Works and Permanent Improvements	Other Expenditure (including Management)	Woods and Plantations	General		Total Expenditure	Net Income
					Churches and Schools (including Works)	Pensions, Compassionate Allowances, Charities and other General Payments		
£ 8,442	£ 6,104	£ 14,445	£ 1,936	£ 4,784	£ 2,045	£ 1,646	£ 39,402	£ 7,124
7,032	6,068	11,892	1,764	4,193	1,140	1,707	33,796	16,511
7,547	6,804	15,803	1,878	4,065	1,901	1,854	39,852	15,017
7,688	5,868	17,841	2,228	4,224	1,127	1,821	40,797	12,735
9,514	6,587	16,517	1,974	4,456	1,209	1,564	41,821	10,442
8,048	6,323	15,723	1,955	3,883	640	2,471	39,043	13,054
7,892	7,799	16,459	2,360	4,294	745	2,877	42,426	9,666
7,735	5,782	15,583	2,304	3,864	498	2,031	37,797	14,163
7,217	5,997	9,373	2,272	3,840	3,177	2,882	34,758	14,751
6,948	6,714	11,254	2,191	3,666	8,465	3,054	42,292	5,617
6,706	6,926	8,697	3,010	3,418	11,761	2,727	43,245	8,854 Deficit 7,531
6,691	11,322	12,941	3,163	3,376	15,853	2,606	55,952	Deficit 14,520
7,117	14,565	10,342	4,131	3,329	23,281	3,474	66,239	
5,752	13,709	5,892	4,643	3,610	8,897	3,146	45,649	7,854
7,032	9,996	2,065	3,944	2,937	4,968	3,841	34,783	12,434
6,850	12,538	2,236	3,266	2,525	4,855	4,124	36,394	10,783
7,314	11,279	3,471	3,037	3,383	5,958	5,936	40,378	11,484
6,975	10,050	1,229	3,632	3,136	3,967	8,800	37,789	17,008
7,882	5,129	5,727	3,754	3,285	2,673	7,681	36,131	21,568
7,538	11,001	6,343	3,802	3,454	3,606	7,986	43,730	13,338
7,920	170,561	203,833	57,244	73,722	106,766	72,228	832,274	217,403

Deficits .. 22,051

£195,352

INCOME

Year	Acreage			Rents received	Woods and Plantations	Income from other Sources
	Estate	Woods and Plantations	Total			
	Acres	Acres	Acres	£	£	£
1876	32,820	4,292	37,112	47,838	8,044	733
1877	32,909	4,277	37,186	52,018	7,290	598
1878	32,842	4,289	37,131	52,397	6,819	307
1879	32,860	4,287	37,147	29,882	4,869	476 [1]
1880	32,855	4,286	37,141	40,186	4,886	2,736 [1]
1881	30,942	4,274	35,216	39,771	6,390	6,773 [1]
1882	28,924	4,130	33,054	40,876	5,744	17,755 [1]
1883	26,769	3,936	30,705	39,761	5,966	10,652 [1]
1884	25,772	3,898	29,670	36,149	6,388	5,977 [1]
1885	25,979	3,897	29,876	25,614	2,999	8,148 [1]
1886	25,979	3,897	29,876	33,762	2,913	6,391 [1]
1887	25,992	3,879	29,871	22,877	3,556	5,184 [1]
1888	25,901	3,891	29,792	28,322	3,308	3,671 [1]
1889	25,842	3,892	29,734	32,486	3,414	5,502 [1]
1890	25,842	3,891	29,733	31,451	3,394	2,823 [1]
1891	25,841	3,891	29,732	29,165	3,088	1,461 [1]
1892	28,042	3,977	32,019	30,956	3,042	2,031 [1]
1893	28,186	3,980	32,166	26,938	4,578	228 [1]
1894	28,179	3,985	32,164	23,366	4,612	1,355 [1]
1895	28,274	4,000	32,274	23,843	5,395	2,882 [1]
				687,658	96,695	85,683

EXPENDITURE *(excluding Store-yard, Brick-kiln, and Establishments)*

..xation	Repairs and Maintenance	New Works and Permanent Improvements	Other Expenditure (including Management)	Woods and Plantations	General		Total Expenditure	Net Income
					Churches and Schools (including Works)	Pensions, Compassionate Allowances, Charities, and other General Payments		
£	£	£	£	£	£	£	£	£
7,335	8,635	10,196	3,600	3,715	3,197	8,022	44,700	11,915
7,362	10,576	9,283	4,300	3,372	11,324	2,286	49,003	10,903
7,908	7,253	8,153	3,815	3,219	5,846	3,003	39,197	20,326
8,209	6,099	7,949	10,714 [1]	2,954	8,312	3,167	47,404	Deficit } 12,177
8,273	6,196	10,781	15,371 [1]	3,195	5,726	3,507	53,049	Deficit } 5,241
8,227	6,169	3,934	17,609 [1]	3,303	2,150	3.014	44,406	8,528
7,486	5,046	4,867	24,530 [1]	3,122	1,309	2,763	49,123	15,252
7,233	8,402	4,830	12,669 [1]	3,044	2,226	2,307	40,711	15,668
6,619	5,174	7,298	13,212 [1]	2,716	1,632	3,593	40,244	8,270
6,535	4,036	4,124	13,690 [1]	2,294	4,379	2,414	37,462	Deficit } 701
6,776	4,125	3,422	10,623 [1]	2,268	6,815	1,980	36,009	7,057
6,459	3,295	1,853	8,953 [1]	2,603	8,267	3,762	35,192	Deficit } 3,575
6,354	3,307	1,649	9,490 [1]	2,390	2,421	2,235	27,846	7,455
6,107	3,202	4,825	7,581 [1]	2,563	3,029	3,140	30,447	10,955
5,943	3,365	4,920	5,681 [1]	2,436	1,725	3,134	27,204	10,464
5,866	3,454	1,492	5,323 [1]	2,308	2,698	2,105	23,246	10,468
6,690	3,529	1,552	3,738 [1]	2,274	3,281	8,600	29,664	6,365
6,534	6,188	5,733	3,987 [1]	3,817	847	5,436	32,542	Deficit } 798
6,428	7,994	6,312	6,855 [1]	3,952	2,064	5,460	39,065	Deficit } 9,732
6,237	7,675	4,458	7,352 [1]	4,694	2,747	5,687	38,850	Deficit } 6,730
99,081	113,720	107,631	189,093	60,229	79,995	75,615	765,364	143,626

...ms in hand.

Deficits . . 38,954

£104,672

Q

SUMMA1

INCOME

Year	Rents received	Woods and Plantations	Income from other Sources	Total Income
	£	£	£	£
1816 to 1835	600,584	185,725	20,570	806,87
1836 „ 1855	664,579	229,165	17,134	910,87
1856 „ 1875	872,722	138,307	16,597	1,027,62
1876 „ 1895	687,658	96,695	85,683	870,03
	2,825,543	649,892	139,984	3,615,41

EDS AND BUCKS

EXPENDITURE

Taxation	Repairs and Maintenance	New Works and Permanent Improvements	Other Expenditure (including Management)	Woods and Plantations	General		Total Expenditure	Net Income	Per Centage of Net Income to Gross Income	Average Annual Net Income
					Churches and Schools (including Works)	Pensions, Compassionate Allowances, Charities, and other General Payments				
£	£	£	£	£	£	£	£	£	£	£
)0,886	188,871	31,231	68,854	—	3,028	15,774	408,644	398,235	49%	19,911
)6,293	148,674	194,652	44,881	63,935	8,847	28,622	625,904	284,974	31%	14,248
17,920	170,561	203,833	57,244	73,722	106,766	72,228	832,274	195,352	19%	9,767
)9,081	113,720	107,631	189,093	60,229	79,995	75,615	765,364	104,672	12%	5,234
24,180	621,826	537,347	360,072	197,886	198,636	192,239	2,632,186	983,233	27%	12,290

From 1816 to 1895—

		£
Total Taxation		524,180
Total Expenditure (other than Taxation)		2,108,006
Total Expenditure		2,632,186
Total Income		3,615,419
Net Income		983,233

Appendix A

THORNEY ESTATE

STATEMENT OF INCOME AND EXPENDITURE

1816 to 1895 inclusive

THORNEY ESTATE

STATEMENT OF INCOME AND

INCOME

Year	Acreage Property let, and Holts and Plantations	Rent received	Income from other Sources	Total Incoi
	Acres	£	£	£
1816	18,809	21,316	1,000	22,316
1817	18,809	21,332	1,028	22,360
1818	18,809	21,363	1,099	22,462
1819	18,923	21,472	1,053	22,525
1820	18,923	21,562	1,166	22,728
1821	18,932	21,421	1,081	22,502
1822	18,932	17,529 [1]	211	17,740
1823	18,932	17,354	435	17,789
1824	18,932	17,360	445	17,805
1825	18,932	17,455	543	17,998
1826	18,932	17,460	548	18,008
1827	18,932	17,477	478	17,955
1828	18,932	20,909 [2]	621	21,530
1829	18,932	20,955	522	21,477
1830	18,932	21,021	526	21,547
1831	18,932	21,271	882	22,153
1832	18,932	22,149	548	22,697
1833	18,932	22,976	653	23,629
1834	18,914	23,089	703	23,792
1835	18,912	23,328	2,885	26,213
		408,799	16,427	425,226

[1] Rents reduced.　　　　[2] Rents increased.

EXPENDITURE, 1816 TO 1895 (*inclusive*)

EXPENDITURE (*excluding Store-yard and Brickmaking Accounts*)

Taxation	Repairs and Maintenance	New Works and Permanent Improvements	Other Expenditure (including Management)	Total Expenditure	Net Income
£	£	£	£	£	£
2,814	5,780	—	1,793	10,387	11,929
2,029	5,528	—	1,725	9,282	13,073
1,724	5,815	—	1,810	9,349	13,113
1,892	6,281	—	1,735	9,908	12,617
1,878	6,394	—	1,865	10,137	12,591
1,834	5,145	—	1,814	8,793	13,709
1,886	4,610	—	1,952	8,448	9,292
1,682	5,174	—	1,859	8,715	9,074
1,776	4,968	—	1,701	8,445	9,360
1,857	5,698	—	1,863	9,418	8,580
1,855	5,087	—	3,849	10,791	7,217
1,856	5,512	—	1,942	9,310	8,645
1,858	7,148	—	1,939	10,945	10,585
1,851	7,473	—	1,881	11,205	10,272
2,753	8,296	—	2,368	13,417	8,130
2,077	9,524	—	2,503	14,104	8,049
3,640	8,628	—	2,148	14,416	8,281
4,962	7,803	—	3,680	16,445	7,184
					Deficit
19,615	7,559	—	3,959	31,133	7,341
7,612	8,206	—	4,259	20,077	6,136
67,451	180,629	—	46,645	244,725	187,842

Deficit   .   7,341

180,501

INCOME

Year	Acreage Property let, and Holts and Plantations	Rent received	Income from other Sources	Total Incor
	Acres	£	£	£
1836	18,913	23,325	857	24,182
1837	18,608	23,270	575	23,845
1838	18,608	23,282	538	23,820
1839	18,608	24,611	580	25,191
1840	18,608	25,912	485	26,397
1841	18,608	25,916	522	26,438
1842	18,604	25,993	537	26,530
1843	18,604	26,012	423	26,435
1844	18,604	26,057	833	26,890
1845	18,604	26,093	774	26,867
1846	18,604	26,125	784	26,909
1847	18,604	26,241	540	26,781
1848	18,605	26,336	4,168 [1]	30,504
1849	18,605	26,408	2,271 [1]	28,674
1850	18,619	26,563	3,186 [1]	29,749
1851	18,619	25,779	3,019 [1]	28,798
1852	19,067	28,265	2,700 [1]	30,965
1853	19,067	27,595	2,253 [1]	29,848
1854	19,064	27,909	2,415 [1]	30,324
1855	19,064	28,137	2,454 [1]	30,591
		519,824	29,914	549,738

[1] Includes Rates levied for highways.

EXPENDITURE (*excluding Store-yard and Brickmaking Accounts*)

Taxation	Repairs and Maintenance	New Works and Permanent Improvements	Other Expenditure (including Management)	Total Expenditure	Net Income
£	£	£	£	£	£
5,494	5,172	—	3,550	14,216	9,966
6,897	5,734	. —	2,962	15,593	8,252
4,907	5,795	—	3,461	14,163	9,657
4,900	5,526	956	2,789	14,171	11,020
4,892	5,425	1,191	2,148	13,656	12,741
4 888	4,608	147	2,362	12,005	14,433
5,186	4,255	3,867	2,649	15,957	10,573
5,508	4,467	1,478	2,250	13,703	12,732
5,512	3,323	1,834	2,331	13,000	13,890
5,501	3,477	2,133	2,448	13,559	13,308
5,534	3,820	3,790	2,467	15,611	11,298
5,509	3,345	2,336	2,531	13,721	13,060
5,506	3,169	3,464	6,124 [1]	18,263	12,241
7,670	2,731	3,156	5,026 [1]	18,583	10,091
5,456	2,669	3,212	4,587 [1]	15,924	13,825
5,181	2,122	2,648	3,791 [1]	13,742	15,056
9,376	4,071	3,612	5,044 [1]	22,103	8,862
8,170	3,976	4,797	4,286 [1]	21,229	8,619
8,131	3,092	2,855	5,223 [1]	19,301	11,023
10,267	4,899	5,002	4,280 [1]	24,448	6,143
124,485	81,676	46,478	70,309	322,948	226,790

[1] Includes cost of highways.

INCOME

Year	Acreage Property let, and Holts and Plantations	Rent received	Income from other Sources	Total Income
	Acres	£	£	£
1856	19,100	31,373	2,524 [1]	33,897
1857	19,100	34,446	2,487 [1]	36,933
1858	19,100	34,527	2,650 [1]	37,177
1859	19,099	34,306	2,018 [1]	36,324
1860	19,099	34,629	1,960 [1]	36,589
1861	19,105	35,273	1,967 [1]	37,240
1862	19,104	34,670	419	35,089
1863	19,103	34,397	816	35,213
1864	19,069	35,208	1,753	36,961
1865	19,068	34,759	1,632	36,391
1866	19,054	35,082	1,045	36,127
1867	19,054	35,213	1,105	36,318
1868	19,059	35,511	915	36,426
1869	18,970	35,640	817	36,457
1870	18,993	35,710	623	36,333
1871	19,056	36,514	1,346	37,860
1872	19,056	36,448	1,943	38,391
1873	19,082	36,676	1,877	38,553
1874	18,924	36,518	1,856	38,374
1875	18,925	36,817	995	37,812
		703,717	30,748	734,465

[1] Includes rates levied for highways.

EXPENDITURE (*excluding Store-yard and Brickmaking Accounts*)

Taxation	Repairs and Maintenance	New Works and Permanent Improvements	Other Expenditure (including Management)	Total Expenditure	Net Income
£	£	£	£	£	£
9,131	4,776	8,976	6,239 [1]	29,122	4,775
9,576	1,984	10,301	4,320 [1]	26,181	10,752
9,013	2,478	11,118	4,376 [1]	26,985	10,192
9,256	2,812	9,017	4,800 [1]	25,885	10,439
9,415	4,811	9,401	4,495 [1]	28,122	8,467 Deficit 1,541 }
9,394	5,480	19,326	4,631 [1]	38,781	
10,951	4,776	9,642	4,853	30,222	4,867
8,941	8,735	6,023	5,015	23,714	11,499
9,632	2,918	4,163	6,036	22,749	14,212
9,575	3,329	6,191	5,853	24,948	11,443
18,041	4,628	5,434	4,836	32,939	8,188
16,943	5,139	6,524	3,554	32,160	4,158
9,716	8,592	6,125	8,072	32,505	8,921 Deficit 361 }
8,978	6,997	13,291	7,552	36,818	
9,296	5,045	2,558	5,668	22,567	13,766
10,096	6,796	1,160	6,290	24,342	13,518 .
10,271	6,847	498	6,574	24,190	14,201
10,231	3,117	582	8,756	22,686	15,867
10,008	5,761	2,680	8,178	26,627	11,747
10,037	6,849	9,543	8,586	35,015	2,797
08,501	96,820	142,553	118,684	566,558	169,809

[1] Includes cost of highways.

Deficits .   1,902

167,907

THORNEY ESTATE

INCOME

Year	Acreage Property let, and Holts and Plantations	Rent received	Income from other Sources	Total Incom
	Acres	£	£	£
1876	19,252	37,524	1,064	38,588
1877	19,305	37,824	967	38,791
1878	19,306	37,922	822	38,744
1879	19,307	20,515	1,319	21,834
1880	19,310	26,263	768	27,031
1881	19,310	19,989	575	20,564
1882	19,320	36,083	1,038	37,121
1883	19,212	33,918	770	34,688
1884	19,267	33,234	1,122	34,356
1885	19,261	19,835	871	20,706
1886	19,261	29,773	594	30,367
1887	19,261	19,669	1,482 [1]	21,151
1888	19,261	31,188	1,398 [1]	32,586
1889	19,323	29,123	866	29,989
1890	19,370	26,471	578	27,049
1891	19,370	30,609	989	31,598
1892	19,369	23,361	652	24,013
1893	19,368	22,245	456	22,701
1894	19,369	18,030	1,031 [1]	19,061
1895	19,369	20,186	2,009 [1]	22,195
		553,762	19,371	573,133

EXPENDITURE (*excluding Store-yard and Brickmaking Accounts*)

Taxation	Repairs and Maintenance	New Works and Permanent Improvements	Other Expenditure (including Management)	Total Expenditure	Net Income
£	£	£	£	£	£
10,151	4,838	14,091	8,924	38,004	584
10,292	4,072	10,195	9,033	33,592	5,199
10,251	4,969	5,207	7,066	27,493	11,251
10,457	3,442	4,255	5,929	24,083	Deficit 2,249 }
10,490	4,552	4,848	5,665	25,555	1,476
10,591	4,005	4,471	6,076	25,148	Deficit 4,579 }
10,464	3,703	1,404	5,595	21,166	15,955
10,444	3,337	5,511	4,549	23,841	10,847
10,258	3,957	4,133	4,050	22,398	11,958
10,344	3,865	99	4,286	18,594	2,112
10,549	3,822	1,791	4,109	20,271	10,096
10,008	3,264	2,440	6,254 [1]	21,966	Deficit 815 }
10,473	2,824	2,668	4,214 [1]	20,179	12,407
9,919	3,110	3,808	4,772	21,609	8,380
9,439	2,893	2,455	4,128	18,915	8,134
9,477	2,788	370	5,120	17,755	13,848
9,509	2,961	1,710	6,703	20,883	3,130
8,820	3,554	1,308	5,481	19,163	8,538
8,666	2,967	2,616	6,627 [1]	20,876	Deficit 1,815 }
8,568	4,825	2,744	6,499 [1]	22,636	Deficit 441 }
199,170	78,748	76,124	115,080	464,122	118,910

Farms in hand.

Deficits . 9,899

109,011

THORNEY ESTATE

INCOME

Year	Rent received	Income from other Sources	Total Income
	£	£	£
1816–1835	408,799	16,427	425,226
1836–1855	519,824	29,914	549,738
1856–1875	703,717	30,748	734,465
1876–1895	553,762	19,371	573,133
	2,186,102	96,460	2,282,562

!HORNEY ESTATE.

EXPENDITURE (*excluding Store-yard and Brickmaking Accounts*)

Taxation	Repairs and Maintenance	New Works and Permanent Improvements	Other Expenditure (including Management)	Total Expenditure	Net Income	Percentage of Net Income to Gross Income	Average Annual Net Income
£	£	£	£	£	£	Per cent.	£
67,451	130,629	—	46,645	244,725	180,501	42	9,025
24,485	81,676	46,478	70,309	322,948	226,790	41	11,340
08,501	96,820	142,553	118,684	566,558	167,907	23	8,395
99,170	73,748	76,124	115,080	464,122	109,011	19	5,450
99,607	382,873	265,155	350,718 [1]	1,598,353	684,209	30½	8,552

From 1816 to 1895—

Total Taxation	£599,607
Total Expenditure (other than taxation)	998,746
Total Expenditure	£1,598,353
Total Income	£2,282,562
Net Income	£684,209

[1] In column 'Other Expenditure' I have included £15,107 on account of death ities. This added to the total of the taxation column would make £614,714, the ture quoted at page 48, Chapter II.

BEDS AND BUCKS ESTATES

STATEMENT OF INCOME AND EXPENDITURE

IN FURTHER EXPLANATION OF EXTRACTS FROM RETURN

1816 TO 1895

R

In further explanation of Extracts

Other Receipts	1846	1878	1879	1
	£	£	£	
Gravel and Sand . . .	51	75	55	
Old Materials sold . . .	207	101	169	
Dilapidations	—	—	—	
Woburn Town Hall (lettings) .	—	—	—	
Estate Farms in hand—Receipts	—	—	163	2,‹
Return of Income Tax on Remitted Rents . . .	—	—	—	
Leases, Fees	—	—	—	
Interest on Money expended on Draining	433	—	—	
Casual Receipts . . .	141	—	12	!
General (Interest and Sundries)	—	131	77	
As per Return	832	307	476	2,‹

from Return 1816–1895, *p.* 59 of Chapter III.

Other Expenditure (including management) [1]	1846	1878	1879	1895
	£	£	£	£
Salaries and Wages . . .	941	2,191	2,693	2,628
Management (*i.e.* Steward's Incidental and Office expenses, Repairs and Taxation of Agents' Residences) . .	269	923	1,612	1,177
Surveying	114	27	78	3
Rent Audit Expenses . .	456	235	68	—
Cultivation and Allowances to Tenants	48	370	483	790
Fixtures purchased . . .	21	8	46	91
Expenses respecting Encroachment on Aspley Heath . .	122	—	—	—
Gravel and Sand . . .	—	51	28	70
Sundries	—	10	11	66
Estate Farms in hand—Expenditure	—	—	5,695	2,181
Leases Disbursements . .	—	—	—	18
Woburn Town Hall (cleaning, repairs, &c.)	—	—	—	22
Allotments (Repairs, Taxation, and other Expenditure) .	—	—	—	306
As per Return	1,971	3,815	10,714	7,352

[1] From 1879 to 1895 the expenditure under the above heading has been considerably increased by the inclusion of neglected farms taken in hand for cleaning and restoration.

Appendix B

THORNEY ESTATE

STATEMENT OF INCOME AND EXPENDITURE

IN FURTHER EXPLANATION OF EXTRACTS FROM RETURN

1816 TO 1895

In further Explanation

Other Receipts	1846	1878	1879
	£	£	£
Tolls ; Dog in a doublet sluice .	183	35	47
„ Turnpikes . . .	75	—	—
Water Rates	—	131 [1]	130 [1]
Gravel and Sand . . .	—	25	14
Old Materials Sold . . .	—	174	174
Dilapidations	—	—	—
Abbey Rooms (Lettings) . .	—	—	—
Farms in hand—Receipts .	—	—	—
Woods Produce . . .	40	226	172
Casual Receipts . . .	183 [2]	21	608 [4]
Repayments by tenants . .	260 [3]	14	2
General (Interest, Railway Dividends, &c.) . . .	42	197	172
As per Return . .	783	823	1,319

[1] Partly received from town residents, partly from His Grace, in respe works and a free supply to cottagers.

[2] Includes receipt for materials supplied to a contractor in repairi tenant's house, £125, and grazing on droves (in later years let to farm tena rents included in " Rents Received "), £34.

[3] Agreed proportion of outlay on new buildings repaid by tenants.

[4] Includes £605 recovered from insurance company in respect of damaε a farmhouse.

. 58 of Chapter III.

; Management)	1846	1878	1879	1895
	£ 1,178	£ 1,729	£ 1,720	£ 1,800
sward's In- Expenses, xation of ce) . .	490	311	570	378
. . .	—	379	—	—
s . .	187	67	37	—
owances to . .	29	65	260	113
. . .	—	18	22	7
ig, Repairs, . .	—	—	—	25
. . .	—	14	11	8
ments .	—	—	—	659
. . .	—	105	119	52
Works .	—	299	327	351
. . .	244	11	22	22
ntra) .	—	14	2	884 [l]
Charges, Gifts, &c.)	339	4,054	2,889	2,199
urn . .	2,467	7,066	5,929	6,498

[l] Valuation of tenant right, &c.

INDEX